THE MEDIATED MUSE

THE MEDIATED MUSE
English Translations of Ovid
1560–1700

Lee T. Pearcy

ARCHON BOOKS
1984

PA
6537
·P37
1984

Printed in the United States of America

The paper in this book meets the guidelines
for permanence and durability of the
Committee on Production Guidelines for
Book Longevity of the Council on Library
Resources.

Library of Congress Cataloging in Publication Data
Pearcy, Lee T., 1947–
    The mediated muse.

    Bibliography: p.
    Includes index.
    1. Ovid, 43 B.C.–17 or 18—Translations, English.
2. Latin language—Translating into English.
3. Marlow, Christopher, 1564–1593—Style. 4. Sandys,
George, 1578–1644—Style. 5. Dryden, John, 1631–1700—
Style. 6. English poetry—Early modern, 1500–1700—
History and criticism. 7. English poetry—Roman
influences. I. Title.
PA6537.P37   1984   871'.01   84-16895
ISBN 0-208-02056-X

Contents

Acknowledgments

I am grateful to Christopher Logue for permission to quote from *War Music, An Account of Books 16–19 of Homer's Iliad*, by Christopher Logue, Jonathan Cape Ltd. and Penguin Books, London, 1984; to the University of Chicago Press for permission to quote from Richmond Lattimore's translation of the *Agamemnon* in *The Complete Greek Tragedies*, edited by David Grene and Richmond Lattimore, [copyright ©] The University of Chicago Press, 1942; and to Viking Penguin Inc. for permission to quote from *Aeschylus: The Oresteia*, translated by Robert Fagles [copyright © 1966, 1967, 1975 by Robert Fagles] and reprinted by permission of Viking Penguin Inc.

Preface

This book is about the translations of Ovid made by Christopher Marlowe, George Sandys, and John Dryden. Even so some account of its genesis may be of interest. Nearly twenty years ago, at Columbia College, Moses Hadas stimulated my interest in translations, and I thought first of making them. Unaware of how difficult *that* would prove, I repeated the mistakes of previous translators and then began to study their work. Renaissance translations came to seem, as they seem now, different in their premises and their attitudes toward style from translations made since the Renaissance. English literature, moreover, offers an opportunity to study the responses of different translators in different times to a single author, Ovid, whose influence in every period is difficult to exaggerate. Studying the Ovid translations of Marlowe, Sandys, and Dryden is rather like hearing how three composers vary a common theme. Shared material and form heighten the individuality of each artist.

It is for readers and serious students of English literature that I have written this book. Hence—with a twinge of regret—I have translated all Latin quotations and put the original at the foot of the page, except where the Latin is important as Latin. A quotation from Natalis Comes, for example, will be given in English with Latin in the footnote, whereas a quotation from Ovid will be in Latin with a translation below unless its meaning is clear from the context. I have spelled Latin in accordance with modern practice, but in quoting sixteenth- and seventeenth-century English I have made no change except to normalize *i / j*, *u / v*, and long and short *s*.

Most of this book was written between 1979 and 1982, and it is a pleasure to thank those who made the writing possible. The American Council of Learned Societies awarded me a fellowship which allowed me to have a year free from academic duties, and the University Research Institute of the University of Texas at Austin further supported my leave of absence and the publication costs of this book. The Principal and Senior Common Room of Mansfield College showed me a kindness and hospitality that made a year in Oxford not only productive but pleasant. I am grateful also to the librarians and staff of the Bodleian Library and the English Faculty Library at Oxford and of the Humanities Research Center and Perry-Castaneda Library at The University of Texas for their assistance. Parts of chapter 4 have been delivered in somewhat different form at meetings of the Classical Association of the Middle West and South and the American Philological Association; I am indebted to everyone who discussed those papers with me. Prof. Richard G. Peterson read the entire book in manuscript and saved me from many blunders, but not from those in which I have obstinately persisted. Ms. Pamela Carrillo turned an untidy manuscript into an elegant and legible typescript. Kathryn Pearcy did not want to be mentioned in this preface, but to have left her out would have been to conceal my greatest debt.

Introduction
The Problem of Translation

Uebersetzung ist eine Form. Sie als solche zu
erfassen, gilt es zurückzugehen auf das Original.
Walter Benjamin, "Die Aufgabe des Uebersetzers"

Translation is rather like gardening. Everyone can recognize the results of the activity, but attempts to define it or lay down rules for it always fail. What definition, what rule of any use could be applied to Capability Brown and the man who, seed catalogue in hand, gazes at a sunny spot in his backyard, or to Pope's *Iliad* and the instructions in English enclosed with the latest electronic gadget from Japan? The problems of defining translation are in fact the problems of defining any procedure by which natural processes are manipulated on a variety of scales and for a variety of ends. Yet attempts to formulate a theory of translation, or at least to classify the various examples of it, continue to be made. More often than not, these attempts have recapitulated the classical dichotomy between letter and spirit and the threefold division of translation into literal on the one hand, imitative on the other, and some mediating and ideal mode between.[1] Lately, however, there have been indications of a change in theorists' approaches to translation. Translation has ceased to be regarded as a sub-department of literature and has come to be seen as a paradigm for language itself. The transfer of meaning between languages appears as an image, limited and controllable, of the whole traffic of meaning between the world and our understanding.[2]

All theories of translation, classical and modern, have in common a perspective focused on the act of making a translation. Whether intended to prescribe rules for this act or to explain it, these theories are concerned with how to translate, with what happens when someone translates, or with the consequences of doing translation one way as opposed to some other. Translation theory is a theory of action.

There is another way to look at translation, or at least at literary translation, which is what I mean by the word from now on. Literary criticism in the late twentieth century has, or ought to have, the restoration and preservation of literacy as its principal objective. The critic's first question is, How do we read? This should be no less true in criticizing translation than any other mode of literature, but critics have been slow to formulate a method of reading translations.

The difficulties are formidable. I. A. Richards once remarked that a translation from Chinese into English was "the most complex type of event yet produced in the evolution of the cosmos."[3] By keeping rather distant from the truth, this kind of exaggeration allows us to have a better view of it. Translation is indeed a complex act, and the reading of a translation partakes of this complexity. When we read an original work, our response proceeds from only two things: the text of the work itself, and our awareness, which we may of course use in a number of different ways, of the author's personality as a presence in some way behind, and antecedent to, the text. The text mediates between author and reader in a structure that is fundamentally linear.

When we read a translation, on the other hand, our response may be more complex. I say "may be" because it is possible that someone reading a translation could be unaware that it was a translation. The story of the man who insisted that if the King James Bible was good enough for Jesus, it was good enough for him, may be apocryphal, but is contains a truth about one way of reading translations. Most people, however, are at the very least aware that the work which they are reading in translation appears in a form different from that in which it originally existed. In this case their awareness of the mere existence of the original must modify their reading of the translation. A translation realizes one, and only one, possible way of transferring meaning. But the reader's knowledge that he is reading one of several possible realizations of the original will give to what he is reading an air of provisionality and tentativeness. A translation can never have the authority of the original from which it is taken. Even if it is the only form in which we know a work, we are prevented from accepting it as equivalent to the original by our knowledge that other renderings are possible.

> Dear gods, set me free from all the pain,
> the long watch I keep, one whole year awake . . .
> propped on my arms, crouched on the roofs of Atreus
> like a dog.[4]

Is that what Aeschylus's watchman says at the beginning of the *Agamemnon*, what he sounds like? Or is it like this:

> I ask the gods some respite from the weariness of this
> watchtime measured by years I lie awake
> elbowed upon the Atreidae's roof dogwise.[5]

These two translations were published only thirty years apart and within the last half century. If we come away unsatisfied from the ponderous yet elusive syntax of the second passage and the absurd picture of the watchman who, if the first version is to be believed, went without sleep for an entire year while crouching propped on his arms, will Browning's version assuage our dissatisfaction? All translations are provisional, essays at the original rather than reproductions of it.

All the translations considered in this book were made in an age when a translator of Latin could assume that his readers would have some degree of acquaintance with the original work being translated. The reading of a translation made under these circumstances belongs to a third, still more complex category. When a reader not only knows that what he is reading is a translation but also knows the original from which the translation has been made, then his response to the translation is determined by his memory of the original as well as by his simple knowledge that because the original exists, other translations are possible. The original becomes a presence not merely behind the text at hand—that of the translation—but around and through it. Instead of the linear relationship that obtained among author, original work, and reader, a multivalent relationship binds a translation to its readers, the translator, the author of the original, and the work translated. The translation lies at the center of a web of reference whose nodes are the reader, the translator, the original work, and the author. When the reader experiences the translation, he is simultaneously aware of the translation as a creation of the translator and as an image of the original work behind which stands the personality of its author. Unlike an original work, whose meaning at any moment of reading is the product of two personalities, author's and reader's, a translation has its meaning determined by three: author's, reader's, and translator's. When the reader knows or can refer to the original as he reads the translation, then at every point original will be woven into translation. As they draw apart so that he says, "No, this is not like Homer, or Horace," or come together so that he can hardly distinguish the impression made by original from that made by translation, their interaction with each other and with the reader creates a structure of meaning.

Translators have not always been chiefly interpreters whose concern is to reproduce the meaning of an original work for those who cannot understand the language in which it is written. In an age when a translator can depend on his readers' knowledge of the work being translated, he can exploit their knowledge to increase the complexity of their response to his work. This increase in complexity compensates for a reduction in the artist's freedom of choice. A translator is not his own master. No matter how far he strays from the sense, style, and shape of his original, it is always there. When Christopher Logue, turning Book 19 of the *Iliad* into English, writes this:

> The chariot's basket dips. The whip
> fires in between the horses' ears,
> and as in dreams or at Cape Kennedy they rise,
> slowly it seems, their chests like royals, yet,
> behind them in a double plume the sand curls up,

he is only rattling his chains.[6] Simply by calling his work by the name of its original, a translator invites comparison from those who are able to compare, and those readers will inevitably respond to a work so named in a different, and more complex, way from that in which they respond to an original work. If we know Homer in Greek, or even that Homer wrote in Greek, we cannot, except by an effort of will so demanding as to make reading and criticism impossible, persuade ourselves that any English text is Homer.

The translator, in effect, gives up freedom to write what he wants in return for the chance to exploit a complex set of references. This bargain has two consequences. One is that theory plays a larger role in the history, criticism, and practice of translation than in other departments of literature. Translations are places to test theories, not only theories of the best relation between original and translation but also more general theories of literary practice, versification or diction, and, as has happened recently, general theories of language itself.

Another, related consequence is that external ideas, doctrines, and dogmas tend to have an influence on translation more readily seen than their influence on original composition. Just as translation easily becomes a testing ground for literary theory, so it becomes a sounding board for nonliterary ideas. The best translators are creators of original literature as well, and it is frequently difficult for such writers to subordinate their personalities to others'. Yet a translator must yield control over the substance of his work to his original author. Again, in compensation for this loss of freedom the translator may increase the complexity of his artifact by adding ideas and allusions to its framework. It is not only a desire to increase the complexity of the work which prompts these additions but a desire to seize the original work and make it over into the new language. Because the original work is necessarily remote from the language and culture of the translation, the translator may find it easy, or inevitable, to pull the original toward his own time and place as well as into his own language. Many have yielded to the temptation to make Euripides' *Trojan Women* into a play about their wars, in Vietnam or Spain, or to assimilate Aristophanes to the style of light opera, musical comedy, or burlesque. But the added ideas, which have their definitive expression in the language and culture of the translator, stand out against the otherness of the original. This contrast is all the more apparent in the case of works from classical antiquity, whose language and culture alike confront the English-speaking reader with a strangeness that demands to be coped with because it is at bottom sameness—like the reaction of twins who, separated at birth, meet after the passage of much time in diverse places.

This book is about the ways in which ideas of literature and the world appear in translations of Ovid made in England between 1560, when the earliest printed translation of any portion of Ovid appeared, and 1700, the death of Dryden. During this period ideas which to us seem inappropriate or irrelevant to Ovid have a perceptible influence on translations of his work. Although it is difficult to give a name and precise definition to the group of ideas whose influence will be traced here, they belong to that interconnected group of Pythagorean, Hermetic, and Neoplatonic doctrines which play a prominent role in Renaissance thought.[7] After this period, for reasons which will be traced in the chapters on Dryden, these ideas cease to have the same kind of importance in translations.

The presence of these ideas in the text of a translation affects our reading of the translation, and that effect is the other subject of this book. When we understand the concepts which a trans-lator has brought to his work, features of it which may have seemed disconnected or unintelligible will fall into place. The rigidity of Marlowe's line-for-line version of Ovid's *Amores*, which seems so at odds with his other works, becomes intelligible when we examine it with the aid of Renaissance numerology. Marlowe left no clue on how to read it except the work itself, but in the case of Sandys's translation of the *Metamorphoses* we have the advantage of a commentary and apparatus in which the translator sets out his concept of the work translated. Our reading of both Marlowe's and Sandys's translations and our understanding of the context and direction of their work will be changed by our application to the text of ideas which, although they have no direct expression in the text, entered into its composition and left their mark on its form. How to make these ideas part of a reading of these translations is the question to be worked out in detail in the following chapters.

If in reading Sandys's and Marlowe's translations of Ovid we ignore the presence and influence of Pythagorean, Hermetic, and

Neoplatonic ideas, we diminish the complexity of the texts and do them a disservice. That complexity of reference was contrived by the translator in compensation for the loss of the freedom or task of inventing new matter, and by ignoring the complexities of a work we read it wrongly. When we come to Dryden's translations, both the function of external ideas in translations and the goal of translation have changed. Instead of drawing on an external system of ideas, correspondences, and analogies to validate its claim to the reader's attention, translation begins to appeal to internal systems. Style, rhetoric, and the nature and degree of a translation's relation to its original become the only tests of worth. Dryden's translations and criticism did not begin or cause this development, but they did consolidate it and give it definitive expression. In so doing, Dryden prefigured the modernist view that style is all that matters in literature. This view may be showing signs of strain; even so, when we read a translation today, we test it by its style and by its relation to the original. Our way of reading translations has been determined by the cogency and defining power of Dryden's statement of the nature of translation. Hence it is a mistake, or at least a failure to appreciate a clearly signaled aspect of the work and the translator's intentions, if we read translations made before Dryden in the same way that we read translations made after Dryden.

Behind or among the translations which are the subject of this book stands the shifting figure of Ovid. Our reading of Ovid, as distinct from our reading of translations of Ovid, has changed greatly in the past twenty-five years. A new appreciation of the merits of rhetoric, a tolerance of freedom of sexual expression, a willingness to see wit as compatible with seriousness, and a certain fondness for the grotesque and *outré* have ousted the nineteenth century's view of Ovid as frivolous, shallow, and not somehow to be trusted or enjoyed, and restored him to his place as a major poet.[8] But the Ovid who is a major poet for us is not the Ovid who was a major poet for Sandys and Marlowe. It requires some effort to recover an Ovid who was important as an authority on matters of fact, one whose status as a poet came not only from what we think of as poetic excellence but also from the fact that what he said was in an absolute sense true. For

Sandys, and to a lesser extent for Marlowe, Ovid was important because he reflected, preserved, and conveyed the truth whose origin was in God and whose image could be seen in the order of the world. It is this Neoplatonic Ovid whose mark can be seen in many pre-Drydenic translations.

No one nowadays reads any ancient author in this way, and if anyone did it is likely that Ovid would be the last author so read. The faint incongruity in our minds of Ovid as scripture makes it all the more important for us to seek out the traces that such a reading of him has left in translations. If we accept the view that every reading alters and shapes the collective perception of a work, that Dante and Milton determine the shape of Virgil for us as much as Virgil determined theirs, then the recovery of another reading of Ovid, one which has been preserved in translations, will not only improve our understanding of the translations, it will also enrich our reading of Ovid himself.

The main subject of this book, however, is how to read translations of Ovid made by Marlowe, Sandys, and Dryden. Marlowe and Sandys represent, in very different ways, the translators of an age when what we think of as nonliterary ideas were as important as stylistic considerations in determining the choices, whether of large-scale design or detail, made by a translator. As Dryden defines the shift toward internal, stylistic criteria for the translator's decisions, so he illustrates it. But before we can begin to consider the influence of Pythagorean and Hermetic ideas on Marlowe's translations from the *Amores*, we must set those translations against the background of other early versions of Ovid and of Elizabethan conventions of reading. What had been done, and what was it possible to do?

1

Marlowe
The Well Agreeing File

The decision to turn some 2,400 lines of Latin into the same number of English lines, and to shape those lines into heroic couplets, is not one to be made on a whim, or without examination of one's predecessors in the same craft. Whether Christopher Marlowe made his translation of Ovid's *Amores* early in his career, as defects of style and misunderstandings of Latin along with subject matter congenial to an undergraduate have suggested, or late, as some verbal parallels with *Hero and Leander* hint, he would have looked for previous translations of Ovid.[1] He would have found a group of translations made in the 1560s or early 1570s. All of Ovid's major works had been Englished, except for the amatory poems. Here was a clear field. (Thomas Blenerhasset's version of *Remedia Amoris*, done while the translator was at Cambridge, seems never to have been printed.) Further, the old translations were beginning to wear, as translations will after two or more decades. By 1590, new developments in style and new ways of reading the ancient authors had made it possible to translate a new Ovid.[2]

Marlowe would have found no printed translation of any part of Ovid earlier than *The Fable of Ovid treting of Narcissus*, which appeared anonymously in 1560. The work is sometimes attributed to Thomas Howell because of the words "Finis. Quod. T. H." which appear at the end. In fact, the initials are probably those of Thomas Hackett, the printer.[3] Lines 342–510 of Book 3 of the *Metamorphoses*, the well-known story of Narcissus and the nymph Echo, become one hundred ninety-two lines in "poulter's measure"—alternate iambic hexameter and heptameter in rhyming couplets. The translation is followed by a lengthy moralization of the kind which had been inseparable from the vernacular Ovid for centuries. Narcissus exemplifies the sin of pride, Echo represents flattery, and moral exempla are adduced from classical antiquity supported by the authority of the Old Testament and medieval and Renaissance literature.

The translation itself displays the faults that have come to be identified with poulter's measure: the tendency toward an unvaried jogging rhythm, the inevitable pause in each couplet after the third foot of the first line and the fourth of the second, and the clogging of the line with monosyllables even as it is retarded by inversions.[4]

> For twentye yeares and one, Narcissus death escaped
> What tyme no chylde was seene so fayre, nor yong man
>   better shapyd,
> A nomber both of men and maydes, did hym desire,
> But bewtye bente with proude dysdayne, had set hym
>   so on fyre
> That nether those whome youthe in yeares, had made
>   his make
> Nor pleasaunte damsels freshe of heue, could wyth him
>   pleasure take.

To these we may add an uncertainty over meter. The fourth line of the translation, for example, falls between two hexameters and ought therefore to be a heptameter: "A chyld even then whom love had lyked well." The translator sometimes varies the iambic movement of his lines by inserting unstressed syllables, especially the third person singular ending "-eth", but the effect is seldom pleasing: "Wythe dobling sound the wordes she heareth, and sendeth againe with screch."[5]

The anonymous translator's Latin, like Marlowe's, was not always adequate to the demands of translating Ovid. Lines 37–38, "None other wyse then as the nerer fyre dothe lye / To brimstone matters mete to borne to flayme doth more applye," give the definite impression that the author did not understand much beyond the first three words of *non aliter quam cum summis* *circumlita taedis / admotas rapiunt vivacia sulphura flammas.* *

For all these faults, *Narcissus* sometimes attains a kind of beauty that makes us forget its inadequacies and set aside our desire to compare it unfavorably to other versions:

> A sprynge there was so fayre, that stremes like sylver had
> Whiche nether shepardes happe to fynde, nor gotes that
>   upwarde gad
> Uppon the rocky hyls, nor other kynde of beste,
> With flashyng feete to foule the same, or troble at the
>   leste,
> Wherin them selves to bathe, no byrdes had made repare,
> Nor leffe had fallen from any tree, the water to appeare,
> And eke the trees had kept the sunne, from commynge
>   doune so lowe.[6]

These eight lines have excellences not in the six lines of Ovid that they render. "[G]otes that upwarde gad / Uppon the rocky hyls" adds life and motion to Ovid's *pastae monte capellae*, and the "flashyng feete" of line 80 are not in *fera turbaret.* Alliteration is rare in *Narcissus*, and its use here calls attention to the liveliness in the image.

Sixteenth-century translators, especially those who were translating a work as well known because of its place in the educational system as the *Metamorphoses*, could depend on their readers' knowledge of the original.[7] The translator of *Narcissus* often betrays his dependence by the way in which he preserves the order of ideas in Ovid's Latin at the expense of English syntax, so that the English has no life of its own but functions as a kind of extended gloss on the Latin:

> *adspicit hunc trepidos agitantem in retia cervos*
> This man the fearful hartes, inforcynge to his nettes
> *vocalis nympha, quae nec reticere loquenti*
> The caulying nimphe one daye, behelde that nether ever
>   lettes
> To talk to those that spake, nor yet hath power of speche

---

*   "Not otherwise than as when lively sulphur, smeared around the tips of torches, seizes the flames brought near."

nec prior ipsa loqui didicit, resonabilis Echo.
Before by Ecco this I meane, the dobbeler of skreeche.

The first line and a half of the English follows the Latin word order almost exactly. The English verb "behelde" is necessarily postponed, and the noun "hartes" is repositioned to follow its adjective, "fearful." Only the phrase "one daye" has no direct equivalent in the Latin. "[T]hat nether ever lettes / To talk to those that spake, nor yet hath power of speche / Before" is only slightly more free as a rendering of *quae nec reticere loquenti / nec prior ipsa loqui didicit*. At this point the translator, whose decision to preserve the word order of the Latin has left him faced with *resonabilis Echo*, must add nearly a line of parenthesis capped by a lame rhyme: "by Ecco this I meane, the dobbeler of skreeche."[8]

Not the least interesting aspect of Marlowe's Ovid is the way in which he exploits and plays with this kind of translating, with which he must have been familiar. It would, after all, have been what he had learned to do in school, as these pedagogical instructions show.

> Take *Flores Poëtarum*, and in every Common place make choise of *Ovid's* verses, or if you find any other which be pleasant and easie: and making sure, that your Schollers know not the verses aforesaid, use to dictate unto them as you did in prose. Cause also so many as you would have to learne together, to set downe the English as you dictate.

After translating the dictated passage into English prose, the Elizabethan schoolboys would turn their English prose into Latin prose, and the Latin prose into Latin verse.

> Secondly, to give you, and to write downe all the words in Latine *verbatim*, or Grammatically.
> Thirdly, having just the same words, let them trie which of them can soonest turne them into the order of a verse: which they will presently do, being trained up in the use of the translations; which is the same in Effect.

Extraordinary as it may seem to twentieth-century teachers

imbued with the idea that even the most elementary product of a childish pen is as unique as the personality of its maker, the verses which emerged at the end of this line of translation and re-translation were expected to be identical or nearly identical to the verses of Ovid with which the chain began.

> And then lastly, reade them over the verses of *Ovid*, that they may see that themselves have made the very same; or wherein they missed: this will much incourage and assure them.[9]

Like the translator of *Narcissus*, the Elizabethan schoolboy translated by assuming an essential word-for-word equivalence between original and translation. To move from prose to verse it was necessary only to juggle the words around.

Marlowe may seem at first to be following the same procedure. His word order is often Latinate, sometimes unintelligibly so, but examination of the Latin shows that he is not always copying the actual word order of the original. In "Hector to arms went from his wives embraces, / And on *Andromache* his helmet laces" (*Amores* 1.9, 35–36), it is necessary to refer to Ovid's Latin to see that "Andromache" is subject of "laces": *Hector ab Andromaches conplexibus ibat ad arma, / et galeam capiti quae daret, uxor erat.* But Marlowe's involuted word order, though it does evoke a Latin original, does not reflect the order of the words in Ovid's couplet; *ibat ad arma*, in fact, is closer to normal English word order than Marlowe's "to arms went."

When we read Marlowe's version of the *Amores* we are always aware that we are reading a translation. A couplet like (to pick an example quite at random) "Behold Cypassis, wont to dress thy head, / Is charg'd to violate her mistress' bed" (2.7, 17–18) not only sounds Latinate, it begs to be turned back into Latin. Even the constructions are laid out for us; "Behold Cypassis" will surely be rendered with *ecce*, and "Is charg'd to violate" alerts us to use a passive verb and infinitive. A look at Ovid's Latin, however, reveals at least one surprise: *novum crimen*, the object of *ecce*, is not translated by Marlowe: *Ecce, novum crimen: sollers ornare Cypassis / obicitur dominae contemerasse torum.* So it goes as we read on. Sometimes Marlowe will use a Latinate word order which is yet not the order of Ovid's Latin; sometimes he will omit

Ovidian ideas in his translation, sometimes add ideas of his own.

For an Elizabethan reader taught by the system of translation and re-translation described by Brinsley, a translation ought to evoke an original, and the original evoked ought to correspond in detail as well as in outline to the original translated. So it is with the anonymous version of the story of Narcissus; set Ovid beside translation, and there will be few surprises, few words in the Latin that are not represented in the English. With Marlowe's Ovid it is far otherwise. If we know the original or consult it, then the translation creates in our mind a constant tension as we attempt, in couplet after couplet, to reconcile expectation with performance, the Ovid we know with the Ovid Marlowe gives us.

Marlowe's exploitation of the way in which his audience would have been taught to read Latin verse provides a clear illustration of the translator's use of complexity of manner to make up for his loss of control over matter. It was no new thing to use Latin word order to evoke an original; the translator of *Narcissus* had done that. Marlowe's achievement was to use Latin word order to create a supposititious original, one which did not correspond at every point to Ovid. This second, ghostly Latin text, whose presence depends on the reader's habitual method of reading Ovid's more full-blooded work, shimmers around Marlowe's translation and, when it is perceived, blurs the outlines of Ovid. A line-for-line translation places severe constraints on its maker. All opportunity for him to express his will and intention or to impose his own order on the material seems lost. On a casual reading Marlowe seems further to efface his own personality by giving us a translation which by its Latinate diction deliberately invites us to merge it with its original. But when we attempt, as Elizabethan readers might have done, to reconstruct that original, we find that Marlowe has hidden it away by merging it with a shadowy second text. The paradoxical effect of Marlowe's special kind of literalness is to deny the original the importance it usually has in literal translation and to place the imprint of his choice of words on every line. Hardly any trace of an artistic personality corresponding to "T. H." can be found in *Narcissus*, but Marlowe asserts his authority as a stylist throughout his version of the *Amores*.

Arthur Golding's translation of the *Metamorphoses*, four books of which had appeared in 1565, the whole in 1567, would have shown Marlowe little to imitate. There is, in fact, no clear evidence that he read Golding at all, but the work's popularity makes it a safe assumption that he did.[10] In transforming Ovid's 12,000 hexameters into 14,000 fourteeners, Golding showed himself a better Latinist than Marlowe; for example, he correctly renders Ovid's *ventos abigoque vocoque, / vipereas rumpo verbis et carmine fauces* (7.202–4) as "By charmes I raise and lay the windes, and burst the viper's jaw." Marlowe's most famous howler is a botch of a similar line from the *Amores: carmine dissiliunt abruptis faucibus angues* (2.1, 25) becomes "Snakes leape by verse from caves of broken mountains."[11]

Golding handles the fourteener with a certain real grace; its tendency to break apart after the fourth foot is mitigated by enjambment, as in these lines from the story of Arachne at the beginning of Book 6:

> And therewithall she purposed to put the Lydian Maide
> Arachne to hir neckverse who (as had to hir bene saide)
> Presumed to prefer hir selfe before hir noble grace
> In making cloth. This Damsell was not famous for the
>   place
> In which she dwelt, nor for hir stocke, but for hir Arte.
>   Hir Sier
> Was Idmon, one of Colophon, a pelting Purple Dier.
> Her mother was deceast: but she was of the baser sort,
> And egall to hir Make in birth, in living, and in port.

Like most translators, Golding emphasizes some features of his author at the expense of others; he is, in fact, inheritor of the medieval tradition of Ovidian interpretation, as the epistle with which he concludes his work shows: "Arachnee may example bee that folk should not contend / Ageinst their betters, nor persist in error to the end." He looks back to *Ovide moralisé* as much as he looks ahead to the Ovid of the next generation. In his preface he expounds the moral interpretation of Ovid's work, but the interpretation must stand apart from the work itself, and the reader of Golding's Ovid, unlike the reader of Caxton's, must construe the fables for himself:

I know these names [of pagan supernatural beings] to
  other things oft may and must agree
In declaration of the which I will not tedious bee.
But leave them to the Readers will to take in sundry wyse,
As matter rysing giveth cause constructions to devyse.

In his translation Golding is concerned to convey Ovid's stories
in all their wealth of detail and elaboration. He glosses difficult
words and mythological allusions, so that *carmina Aonidum*
becomes "the Muses learned song," and he expands on Ovid in
order to simplify terse expressions, so that *tum secum* becomes
"And thereupon within herself this fancie did arise," or merely
to fill out a line, as when *aequa viro fuerat* becomes "And egall
to her Make in birth, in living, and in port." By such expansions
Golding manages to produce an effect similar to the *copia*, the
elaboration of detail, that is one of the strengths Ovid drew from
his rhetorical training and turn of mind.

Golding fails, however, to convey anything of the quality
which balances *copia* in Ovid's rhetoric: its terseness. Again at
the beginning of the sixth book, "It is no matter for to prayse:
but let our selfe devise / Some thing to be commended for: and
let us not permit / Our Majestie to be despisde without revenging
it" conveys very well the meaning of *laudare parum est,
laudemur et ipsae / numina nec sperni sine poena nostra sinamus.*
It does not, however, convey the interaction of
laudare . . . laudemur, or the play of nasal and sibilant consonants
in *numina nec sperni sine poena nostra sinamus.* Ovid wrote long
poems by single lines. The fondness for the *sententia,* or
epigrammatic statement summarizing a situation, and the
attention to the structure and balance of words and sounds within
a line were Ovid's legacy—some would say his curse—to later
Latin poetry; they were also among the qualities that attracted
Marlowe to him. Golding recognized the attractiveness of Ovid's
style but chose not to imitate it:

Wherein although for pleasant style, I cannot make
  account
To match myne author, who in that all other dooth
  surmount:
Yit (gentle Reader) doo I trust my travail in this cace

May purchace favour in they sight my dooings to
   embrace.[12]

Marlowe did seek to match his author in "pleasant style." He
was the first (for Chaucer's couplet is far different) to use the
closed iambic pentameter couplet for sustained composition, and
his choice of it can be seen as an attempt to capture something
of the balanced, pointed style, the careful placing of words within
a line, that Ovid uses in the *Amores*.[13] Sometimes we can set Ovid's
Latin beside Marlowe's English and see clearly what the translator
was imitating. At 1.2, 21, for example, "What needes thou warre,
I sue to thee for grace, / With armes to conquer armlesse men
is base," the balance of "warre" at the caesura with "grace" at
the line's end reflects Ovid's juxtaposition of *bello* with *veniam
pacemque* in *nil opus est bello: veniam pacemque rogamus*, and
the picking up of "armes" in "armlesse" reflects *armis* and
inermis in *nec tibi laus armis victus inermis ero*.* To achieve this
reflection Marlowe has had to turn Ovid's line from a statement
by the narrator of the poem into an impersonal, but still Ovidian,
sententia. That this way of translating does not strike us as
unusual—for is it not a translator's duty to approximate the style
of his author?—is an indication of how much our idea of
translation is dominated by concepts that did not become
generally accepted until Dryden articulated them. For a measure
of Marlowe's originality, we need only remember Golding's
handling of *laudare parum est, laudemur et ipsae / numina nec
sperni sine poena nostra sinamus*.

At 1.5, 3, Marlowe's "One window shut, the other open stood"
imitates the movement of Ovid's *pars adaperta fuit, pars altera
clausa fenestrae*. Marlowe's line, like Ovid's, is carefully poised
around a strong caesura, and his postponement of "stood"
corresponds to Ovid's postponement of *fenestrae*. Marlowe has
translated the shape of Ovid's line, and in so doing he has made
Ovid's single window with two shutters into two windows, one
open and one shut.

But instances where Marlowe can be shown to have imitated
a specific feature of a line of Ovid are rare. He found in Ovid

---

* "I, an unarmed man conquered by arms, shall not be something for which
   people praise you."

something that Golding and the other early translators had not sought: tightness, balance, a sense of one word placed to weigh against another. His translation imitates this quality throughout and becomes Ovidian even though it does not copy Ovid at every line or in every feature. Marlowe's version of the *Amores* is, in fact, the first English Ovid to translate style equally with substance and to attempt to give the general effect as well as the specific meaning of its original.

Not that a sense of style had been altogether absent from earlier English Ovids. Thomas Churchyard's *Tristia* of 1572 in thumping, alliterative fourteeners displays that "dalliance with the letter" that sixteenth-century rhetoricians recommended for elegies, epitaphs, and other sad contexts:

> When I the pensive picture see, of darcke and drery night,
> And in my minde beholde the Towne, from whence I
>   toke my flight.
> Or time record, when I did leave, my frendes and dere
>   allyes,
> Then do the dolefull droppes discende, from my sad
>   weeping eyes.
> The day drue on I should depart, as CAESAR wis'd before,
> And flee a farre to partes extreame, and shunne ITALIA
>   shore.[14]

It is easy enough to be amused at this. But we should remember two things: first, "This fatal sing-song, not blank verse or the sonnet, was the form that Surrey's immediate successors took up most enthusiastically. It is in this form that Surrey's verse is most regular metrically, and the regularity is of the peculiar kind that dominated English poetry for twenty years after 1557."[15] Second, Churchyard handles his chosen form masterfully. Gone is the metrical uncertainty that marked the anonymous *Narcissus* of 1560, and which can be seen also in the version in poulter's measure of *Epistulae Heroidum* 16 (Helen to Paris) by Sir Thomas Chaloner (1521–1565).[16] Even the enjambment that gave a certain lightness and grace to Golding's fourteeners of 1567 has been set aside in favor of the unvaried and quite literally enchanting rhythm of four paces, then three, four paces, then three. This regular march of the verse does not for the most part disrupt the syntax; Churchyard's lines read smoothly, and only rarely are we brought up short by contorted syntax like this in his translation of *Tristia* 1.5, 1–4:

> CALLIMACHUS did not so burne, with love to Lyda sent,
> Nor yet so sore PHYLATES had, his heart on BATTIS bent,
> As thee (O mate most true), my breast, within I deeply
>   grave,
> Which worthy are a better not, but happier husband
>   have.

Golding claimed to make no attempt to match Ovid in "pleasant style"; for him, the stories mattered most. For Churchyard style mattered, but the style of his translation is very unlike Ovid's, or Marlowe's.[17]

In the same year that Golding published his complete version of the *Metamorphoses*, George Turberville issued his version of Ovid's *Epistulae Heroidum*, a series of highly rhetorical epistles from mythical and legendary heroines to their lovers. Turberville also translates three of the additional replies written by Ovid's contemporary, Aulus Sabinus.[18] At first glance it might seem that Turberville, not Marlowe, could claim to be the first to attempt to translate Ovid's style equally with his sense. In his appended apology, "The Translator to the captious sort of Sycophants," he remarked on his struggles with Latin:

> For though the thing but slender be in sight
> And vaine to vewe of curious carping skull,
> In mother tongue a forraine speach to write:
> Yet he shall finde he hath a Crow to pull.
> That undertakes with well agreeing file
> Of English verse, to rub the Romaine stile.
>
> Divises of the language divers are,
> Well couched words, and feately forged phrase,
> Eche string in tune, no ragged ryme doth jarre
> With fingers fraught their bookes in everie place;
> So that it is a worke of prayse to cause
> A Romaine borne to speake with English jawes.

It is this difficulty that causes him to speak of taking in hand his "painefull pen" in a prefatory epigram, "The Translator to his Muse."

But when we look at the translations themselves, we find that Turberville is not so much concerned to give us a version of Ovid in an English whose effects are equivalent to the effects of Ovid's Latin as he is to give us Ovid's matter in an English that is vivid and idiomatic—but not intentionally Ovidian. In fact, the difficulties to which he refers in the verses quoted above are the difficulties of moving from Latin to English, not from Ovid to a translation of Ovid. Many Renaissance translators saw translation from the classical languages as a process of appropriation whereby the receptor language was enriched by adopting something of the vocabulary, diction, and idiom of the original language. This view Turberville rejects. The "divises" of Latin seem to him so different from anything possible in English that he does not consider the possibility of producing something like them in English, and when he translates Ovid, he makes no effort to transfer anything of Ovid's style to his translation. When the "Romaine borne" speaks with English jaws, we hear only English.

Nowhere is this Englishing of Ovid clearer than in the homely sayings which pepper Turberville's verses. A fondness for versifying such popular expressions was one characteristic of the fourteeners and poulter's measure of the 1560s and 1570s, and Turberville often turns a plain statement in Ovid into a vigorous aphorism.[19] In Letter 16, "Helen to Paris," Ovid's *Saepe vel exiguo, vel longo murmure dixi, / Nil pudet hunc: nec vox haec mea falsa fuit** becomes "Oft times with whispering wordes unto my selfe I sed: / (This is a shameless guest) my wordes did hit the nayle on hed."

When we turn from the translations in fourteeners (*Epistles* 1, 2, 4, 5, 8, and Sabinus's reply to 1) or poulter's measure (*Epistles* 3, 6, 7, 9, 10, 11, 15, 16, 17, 18, 19, and Sabinus's replies to 2 and 5) to those in decasyllabic verse (*Epistles* 12, 13, 14, 20, and 21), we see no sign that Turberville treated his ten-syllable line as significantly different from his twelve- or fourteen-syllable line. Alliteration is characteristic of his fourteeners,

---

*   "Often in a thin or drawn-out voice I said, 'Nothing makes him ashamed,' and this remark of mine was not false."

A rustick let me be, so I not passe the bounde
Of honest shame, and in my life no cankred crime be
    founde,
So I in fayned looke doe cloake no churlish cheare:
Nor in my face no grimme disdaine nor bended browe
    appeare.[20]

and of his decasyllables,

But hedlong hence thou wentst, & wished winde
Of seamen not of me, they sayles allurde:
That gale was meet for Mariners, unfit
For those that love.[21]

Turberville allows more trochaic and anapestic substitutions in his decasyllables than in his other measures, as in "Shall I in purple Robe and Silkes be clad, / And he wage warre under the walles of Troie?" (p. 75v) or "But sore I dreade, and looke how oft I minde / The lamentable warre, and fearefull flight" (p. 76r). In all his verse he treats proper names as extra-metrical, unless they can be easily made to fit: "Did TAENARIS thee with porte relieve thy painefull plight to ease?" (p. 98v).

All in all, Turberville gives the most pleasure of any of the pre-Marlowe Ovids. His English, vivid and almost always clear, moves smoothly along; his "dalliance with the letter" delights without becoming obtrusive, as it often did in Churchyard's verses; and in the end we can agree that he has attained his aim of making a Roman speak with English jaws. This aim was not Marlowe's. He sought to make his English sound from Roman jaws, to accommodate English to Ovid, not Ovid to English. Marlowe's choice of the closed iambic pentameter couplet reveals his bold originality and sensitivity to the possibilities inherent in a form, for the heroic couplet is in fact the English form whose inner dynamics are closest to those of the Ovidian elegiac couplet with its flexibility and balance, its varied word order, and its inevitable closure.[22] To see this inner resemblance in the 1590s or earlier, when the heroic couplet was in its infancy and Ovidian translation meant for the most part fourteeners or poulter's measure, required more than Latinity and the ability to compose English verse. It required deep understanding of the way two languages work, of the effects realized in one and of the possibilities latent in the other. It required also conviction that the thing could be done.

To see how well Marlowe did it, we need to examine in some detail his handling of Ovid's text in *Amores* 1.2, a poem representative of both Ovid's and Marlowe's manner. It appeared in the selection of ten elegies published with Sir John Davies's *Epigrams* sometime in the 1590s.[23]

Amores 1.2 opens with a question. Why is it, the poet asks, that he can't sleep:

> Esse quid hoc dicam, quod tam mihi dura videntur
>   strata, neque in lecto pallia nostra sedent,
> et vacuus somno noctem, quam longa, peregi,
>   lassaque versati corporis ossa dolent?

The *Amores* are best read in sequence, and after the first poem, in which Cupid prevented the poet from writing epic and turned him to erotic elegy ("When in this workes first verse I trod aloft, / Love slackt my Muse, and made my numbers soft," 1.1, 21–22), there can be little doubt of the reason for the poet's insomnia. We know that the reason can only be love, but the rhetorical question has allowed the poet to establish a setting for the poem—night, his bedroom, him tossing and turning—and to portray with a deft psychological sketch in the next lines the process of gradual realization. Surely he would know if it were love that troubled him—or would he? *[N]am, puto, sentirem, si quo temptarer amore— / an subit et tecta callidus arte nocet?* The slow, deliberative pace of this couplet's hexameter, with its spondaic center, reflects the poet's slowly dawning awareness of the cause of his condition, and the faster, dactylic movement of the pentameter mirrors the speed with which he understands.

Once the cause is known, deliberation is brief and resistance halfhearted. Do we yield? We do.

> sic erit: haeserunt tenues in corde sagittae,
>   et possessa ferus pectora versat Amor.
> cedimus, an subitum luctando accendimus ignem?
>   cedamus: leve fit, quod bene fertur, onus.[24]

Three examples follow in three couplets: shaken torches blaze up more brightly, oxen who balk at the yoke are beaten more often, the fierce horses get the harsh curbs. Since resistance is useless, the poet surrenders to Cupid; Love's latest captive sues for peace:

> en ego, confiteor, tua sum nova praeda, Cupido;
>   porrigimus victas ad tua iura manus.
> nil opus est bello: veniam pacemque rogamus;
>   nec tibi laus armis victus inermis ero.

With this military metaphor the prelude is over, and Ovid begins a fantasia on the Triumph of Love. This theme he took from Propertius 3.1, 9–14; the scale and tone are entirely his.

This fantasia serves three purposes: First, it presents a new and original combination of the elegists' old themes of the *militia Amoris*, the military service of Love, and the *servitium Amoris*, Love's service. If a soldier's life is terribly hard, then so is a lover's and in similar ways. Who, the elegists say, can assert that one is better than the other?[25] And a lover, whatever his station, has no more freedom than a slave. Second, the depiction of Love's triumph allows Ovid to use several images favored by the Augustan regime—the triumph itself, Venus and her kin, Pudor, even Bacchus—in a way which, while it perhaps ought not to be called anti-Augustan, would certainly have surprised the advocates of a grave, stately, public-spirited, and imperial Augustanism. Cupid's frivolous triumph parodies, detail by detail and couplet by couplet, one of Augustanism's sacred rites.[26] Third, Love's triumph takes us away from the world we know, the world apprehended by our senses, into a world entirely of Ovid's creation, where sense-experience is unreliable or inapplicable. It is the world of the *Metamorphoses*—indeed, of most of Ovid's poetry.

Ovid's description of Cupid's triumph occupies a little more than half the poem (vv. 23–49). The god, in a chariot given him by his stepfather Vulcan and drawn by the doves of his mother, Venus, will lead along the youths and maidens who are enslaved to him:

> necte comam myrto, maternas iunge columbas;
>   qui deceat, currum vitricus ipse dabit;
> inque dato curru, populo clamante triumphum,

> stabis et adiunctas arte movebis aves.
> ducentur capti iuvenes captaeque puellae:
> haec tibi magnificus pompa triumphus erit.

These three couplets well illustrate Ovid's careful attention to the interconnection of his end-stopped couplets. In line 25 *dato curru* links with *currum...dabit* in line 24. The first two couplets are further joined together by the reference of *aves* in line 26 to *columbas* in line 23, so that the four lines mention in chiastic order doves and chariot, chariot and doves. Metrical shape also joins the two couplets; in each, the hexameter has the so-called penthemimeral caesura in the middle of the third foot, and *necte comam myrto* has exactly the same disposition of dactyl and spondee, ictus and accent, as *inque dato curru* (– u ú – – – –). The two pentameters have each the same arrangement of dactyls and spondees, though to be sure the possibilities for variety are fewer in the second line of an elegiac couplet. Finally, a third couplet, metrically different with its spondaic opening to the hexameter and septhemimeral caesura, as well as its entirely dactylic pentameter, closes this section. The rather colorless pentameter of this last couplet does at least emphasize its summarizing function.

After the lines of general description, the fantasia returns to the poet himself. He goes, wounded, in the train of Cupid's captives, along with *Mens Bona, Pudor*, and whatever else opposes Love's host:

> ipse ego, praeda recens, factum modo vulnus habebo
> et nova captiva vincula mente feram.
> Mens Bona ducetur manibus post terga retortis
> et Pudor et castris quidquid Amoris obest.[27]

Ovid assembles his verse from the unit of the single couplet, itself made of smaller units: the line, phrase, and word. Here *praeda recens* recalls *nova praeda* in line 19, and *vulnus habebo* will recur, as the poet's plight is generalized, in *vulnera multa dabis* at line 44. In the next couplet (vv. 33–34), the multitude's gesture as they stretch out their hands toward Love the conqueror recalls the poet's gesture (*porrigimus victas ad tua iura manus*) at line 20 and prepares for the moment when the spectators become Love's victims too at lines 43–44.

The triumphator, as was usual in a Roman triumph, rides in the center of the procession, preceded by his victims (the poet, Good Intention, and Modesty) and followed by his soldiers (Blandishments, Error, and Madness):

> Blanditiae comites tibi erunt Errorque Furorque
>   adsidue partes turba secuta tuas.
> his tu militibus superas hominesque deosque;
>   haec tibi si demas commoda, nudus eris.[28]

Over the whole scene presides his fond mother:

> laeta triumphanti de summo mater Olympo
>   plaudet et adpositas sparget in ore rosas.

Our attention now returns to the triumphal god himself, his bejeweled wings, his golden hair and car. In his passing he will wound many among the spectators, for he cannot stop his arrows; their very nearness wounds. Such as the triumph of Bacchus over India:

> tu pennas gemma, gemma variante capillos,
>   ibis in auratis aureus ipse rotis.
> tunc quoque non paucos, si te bene novimus, ures;
>   tunc quoque praeteriens vulnera multa dabis.
> non possunt, licet ipse velis, cessare sagittae;
>   fervida vicino flammas vapore nocet.
> talis erat domita Bacchus Gangetide terra:
>   tu gravis alitibus, tigribus ille fuit.

With this last *sententia*, so neatly balanced and perhaps a little frigid, Ovid's account of Love's triumph is over.

There follows what Douglass Parker has called the "Ovidian coda," a short section that turns the poem in a new direction and suggests a new frame of reference.[29] Since, the poet says, I can be part of your triumph, don't waste your resources any further on me—look, here are the weapons of your kinsman, Caesar; *he* protects the conquered with his conquering hand:

> ergo cum possim sacri pars esse triumphi,
>   parce tuas in me perdere victor opes.
> aspice cognati felicia Caesaris arma:
>   qua vicit, victos protegit ille manu.

A concluding irony is packed into the epithet *cognati*, which reminds us that the Julian line claimed to be descended from Venus, and into the anadiplosis of *qua vicit, victos protegit ille manu*. The thing looks like flattery, but would Augustus, public advocate of old-style morality, have been flattered to think of himself as Cupid's cousin, protector of the author of the *Amores*? Nor would *manu qua vicit* have been received with modest blushes; on more than one occasion a sudden indisposition had kept Augustus from personal attendance on the battlefield.[30]

This reading of *Amores* 1.2 has been necessary to show in a general way what Marlowe had before him when he began. A twentieth-century Latinist will, of course, realize possibilities in the text different from those realized by a sixteenth-century Latinist; in particular, our taste for ironies and images and our obsession with finding unifying elements was not shared by earlier readers. They were more apt to be interested in the play of rhetoric and in the visual and allegorical possibilities presented by an imaginary spectacle like Cupid's triumph. Mantegna and Petrarch's *Trionfi* might make a good commentary on Marlowe's version of *Amores* 1.2.[31]

But our concern is with how Marlowe's words work with each other and with Ovid's text. Marlowe's couplets, like Ovid's, are all closed. But if Ovid's couplets are all end-stopped, his lines are not. The difference in shape and movement of the hexameter and pentameter makes the Latin elegiac fall naturally into theme followed by variation, question joined to answer, and the flexibility of Latin word order makes it possible to unify a couplet by postponing into the pentameter a word necessary to complete the sense of the hexameter.[32] Two patterns of this enjambment are especially common in Ovid. In one, the subject of the sentence begun in the hexameter falls at the end of the pentameter (e.g., *acrius invitos multoque ferocius urget, / quam qui servitium ferre fatentur, Amor*); in the other, the main verb is postponed until the beginning of the pentameter (e.g., *inque dato curru, populo clamante triumphum, / stabis et adiunctas arte movebis aves*).

Marlowe did not have these resources. Both lines of his couplet are metrically identical, and English word order allows for less variation than Latin. We have seen also that in using, or suggesting, Latinate word order, Marlowe was attempting to exploit, indeed almost to parody, an Elizabethan notion of translating. Rhyme too might unify a couplet, but, as its disparagers note, it can easily become a thing strained after and tacked on. Marlowe's couplets tend to break apart into self-contained lines.

> What makes my bed seem hard, seeing it is soft?
> Or why slips down the Coverlet so oft?
> Although the nights be long, I sleepe not tho,
> My sides are sore with tumbling to and fro.

Each of these lines is grammatically independent of its neighbor, and it is only logical connection, which of course Marlowe found in Ovid, that groups them into pairs. On the rare occasions when Marlowe does use enjambment, the stimulus for it is usually to be found in Ovid. "With beautie of thy wings, thy faire haire guilded, / Ride golden Love in Chariots richly builded" simply imitates in its positioning of "ride" Ovid's placing of *ibis* in *tu pennas gemma, gemma variante capillos / ibis in auratis aureus ipse rotis*. As Roma Gill observes in considering the opening lines of 1.2, "The dialectical influence of the Metaphysical poets was necessary before, in Pope's hands, the couplet could become an organic part of the poem."[33]

As for the rhyme, "seeing it is soft" has no counterpart in Ovid's Latin, and "tho" as well sounds strained. The first rhyme, however, may have been suggested to Marlowe by the commentary of Dominicus Niger: *Quid esse causae dicam, inquit poeta, rudis adhuc, & tyro in amatoriis castris, quod strata,* quae alioqui sunt mollia, *mihi tam dura & aspera videntur?*[34] In seeking a rhyme, Marlowe's last resource is his own invention. Translating 3.2, 29–30, *talia Milanion Atalantes crura fugacis / optavit manibus sustinuisse suis*, Marlowe selects an alternate name for Milanion so that he can have a rhyme for "these" in "swift Atalanta's flying legs, like these, / Wish in his hands grasp'd did Hippomenes." But in gaining a rhyme he has allowed himself to ruin a line, for "Wish in his hands grasp'd did" is scarcely intelligible, and little more than a word-for-word gloss on *optavit manibus sustinuisse suis*.

Marlowe's failure to make the couplet his unit of composition does not originate in any inability to see beyond the boundaries of a single pair of lines. Continuing in *Amores* 1.2, Marlowe renders Ovid's *nam, puto, sentirem, si quo temptarer amore—/ an subit et tecta callidus arte nocet?* with "Were Love the cause, it's like I shoulde descry him, / Or lies he close, and shoots where none can spie him?" The image of Love waiting in ambush and shooting from cover is not in Ovid's plain *tecta callidus arte nocet.** Marlowe has anticipated the imagery of the next couplet: *sic erit: haeserunt tenues in corde sagittae, / et possessa ferus pectora versat Amor*, gracefully rendered by "T'was so, he stroke me with a slender dart, / Tis cruell love turmoyles my captive hart." But this use of imagery to strengthen and unify his lines may be a matter of chance, not policy, for in the next couplet Marlowe sacrifices an image for a rhyme. *Cedimus, an subitum luctando accendiums ignem? / cedamus: leve fit, quod bene fertur, onus*, becomes "Yeelding or striving doe we give him might, / Lets yeeld, a burden easily borne is light." Ovid can continue the fire image in the next couplet, but Marlowe has lost the opportunity to link couplets with an image and must confine his fire to one pair of lines:

> vidi ego iactatas mota face crescere flammas
>   et vidi nullo concutiente mori;

> I saw a brandisht fire increase in strength,
> Which being not shakt, I saw it die at length.

Le secret d'ennuyer, as Voltaire reminds us, *est de tout dire*. We will not go line by line through the rest of Marlowe's translation of *Amores* 1.2, pausing to smile at admirable couplets or to shake our heads gravely over things that might have been done better. Anthologies of Marlowe's howlers, clinkers, and successes have been made before now. A larger question demands our attention: Why did Marlowe take the pains to produce this labored and uneven version of the *Amores*? Line-for-line translation of a work one-quarter the length of the *Aeneid* does not seem the lightly undertaken pastime of an idle hour.

---

*   "Does he cleverly do his hurt with concealed art."

2

Marlowe
Inexcusable Pythagorisme

The impulse behind Marlowe's decision to translate Ovid may lie in the interests revealed by the first publication of his version of the *Amores*. This slim volume presented along with John Davies's *Epigrams* a selection of ten poems: Book 1, poems 1, 2, 3, 5, 13, and 15; Book 2, poems 4 and 10; and Book 3, poems 6 and 13 (7 and 14 in modern editions of Ovid).[1] The poems appeared in the order 1.1, 1.3, 1.5, 3.13, 1.15, 1.13, 2.4, 2.10, 3.6, and 1.2. One principle of selection was certainly, as Maclure says, "to include some warmly erotic pieces," and 1.5, 2.4, and 3.6 certainly fall into that category. A puritanical judge might place 1.13, 2.10, and 3.13 in the same group, although they are no warmer in their eroticism than many Elizabethan love poems that escaped censure—and the Archbishop of Canterbury's order which appeared in the *Stationers' Register* for 1599, calling in "Davyes *Epigrams*, with Marlowe's *Elegyes*," was, as its order of emphasis indicates, directed mainly at Davies's satirical epigrams. On the other hand, no amount of searching after sex can make 1.1, 2, 3, and 15 anything but poems about poetry, and specifically about the motivation, power, and poetic status of the love elegy. A translator or editor in search of frankly erotic material would have done better to include 2.7 and 8, 15, or 19. We may suspect some principle of selection in addition to a preference for the warmly erotic.

We cannot, of course, know the extent of Marlowe's involvement in the first, fugitive publication of ten elegies. Even the exact date of its publication is unknown.[2] Hence all that follows is to some extent speculation, although I hope that it will make clear the reasons behind my own belief that Marlowe arranged the elegies for the first publication.

A translator who is also a poet works under constant temptation to add his own invention to that of the author whom he is translating, and, if not to improve the original, at least to stamp it with some sign of his presence. In a line-for-line translation into so strict a measure as the heroic couplet, opportunities are limited. Not that Marlowe passes them up altogether; in the previous chapter I argued that his use of Latin word order arose from a desire to establish his stylistic presence as a translator, and throughout his version of the *Amores* we find lines that reveal attitudes and ideas typical of him.[3] But in searching for a means of establishing his poetic presence in *Ovid's Elegies*, Marlowe could have found only one opportunity to display his invention on a large scale. By careful ordering of the poems, he could select and emphasize the ideas and themes that had attracted him to the *Amores* in the first place and thus transform Ovid's collection into his own selection from Ovid. In choice there could be creativity.

In fact, a casual glance at the collection will reveal a pattern in the order of the ten elegies. Marlowe's version of the first poem in Ovid's collection, 1.1, is separated from the second, 1.2, by eight other poems. *Amores* 1.1 and 1.2 are best read in order. Both deal with the power of Love: in 1.1, Cupid overcomes the poet as he is about to write an epic and turns him to elegy, and in 1.2, Cupid marches in triumph through the poet's dreams. Both poems raise the question of the love-poet's role in society, the first by opposing personal elegy to public epic, and the second by exploiting a public image, the triumph, to express private compulsions, and by the ironic introduction of Caesar into its coda. By placing these similar poems at opposite ends of his selection, Marlowe calls our attention to the themes they share and to the order of the intervening elegies.

These eight elegies fall naturally into three groups. The first three poems all deal with the poet's mistress, Corinna.[4] In *Amores* 1.3 the poet announces his fidelity to his mistress. He loves her with unblemished fidelity (*pura fide* 6), and even though his ancestry is humble and his estates small, he is at least a poet. He will yield to no one in fidelity (*nulli cessura fides* 13); he will love only her forever, if fidelity means anything at all: *tu mihi, si qua fides, cura perennis eris.* And he will give her immortality through his poetry, just as poets have given other women immortality—Io, and Leda, and Europa. But all these were loved by the archetypal adulterer, Jove (*et quam fluminea lusit adulter ave*), and at the end of this characteristic coda with its complex ironies we are left less than sure of the poet's single-mindedness.

Amores 1.5, the third poem in Marlowe's selection, is too rich in theme and construction to analyze in full here. The poet, lying on his couch for a siesta, receives a visit from Corinna. He snatches her thin tunic; she puts up a half-hearted resistance, her mind divided between resisting and not wanting to win (*quae, cum ita pugnaret tamquam quae vincere nollet, / victa est non aegre proditione sua*). They make love. No Ovidian irony here, only lusty enthusiasm—until we ponder the insistence on middle states (*mediam horam* 1, *medii dies* 26, the window half open and half shut, Corinna's hair divided on her neck), the emphasis on covering, uncovering, and half-covering, and the epiphanic language in which Corinna's visit is described.[5] What is real here, and what is unambiguous?

Amores 3.13 presents the poet's fidelity in a light different from 1.3. Now the poet has become urbane and less overcome—if indeed he ever was—by passion. He suspects his mistress of infidelity and (since he cannot help loving her) asks only that she not tell him of her love affairs. Here Ovidian irony suffuses the poem, for to ask not to know of something, and to explain in great detail what that something is that you do not wish to know of, is to admit that you know what you don't want to learn.

The first three of the eight central poems in Marlowe's selection, then, form a group. All have as premise the poet's love for a single woman, and two (1.3 and 3.13) present the question of *fides* in contrasting ways. Between them comes a complex poem whose appeal is at once sensual and psychological, combining erotic narrative with presentation of the ambiguous state of mind that may underlie sexual acts. We will take up the next two poems in Marlowe's selection, 1.15 and 1.13, in a moment. The last three, 2.4, 2.10, and 3.6, contrast immediately with the first three. Corinna is out of the picture, and the poet, far from pledging undying loyalty to one woman as he did in

1.3, analyzes at length his compulsion to love many. As with the
first group of three, the first and third poems in this latter group
present contrasting views of the same basic attitude, fidelity in
the former group and promiscuity here. Between the first and
third poems of this latter group also intervenes a poem depicting
an ambiguous state of the erotic mind.

The Renaissance title for 2.4, the seventh poem in Marlowe's
selection, gives a fair summary of its contents: *Quod amet
mulieres, cuiuscunque formae sint*. Marlowe's version is one of
his gayest and most successful, perhaps because Ovid does for
a moment speak with English—and specifically Elizabethan—
jaws. The last few lines may stand in lieu of further analysis:

> If she be tall, shees like an *Amazon*,
> And therefore filles the bed she lies uppon:
> If short, she lies the rounder: to speak truth,
> Both short and long please me, for I love both:
> I think what one undeckt would be, being drest;
> Is she attired, then shew her graces best.
> A white wench thralles me, so doth golden yellowe,
> And nut-brown girles in doing hath no fellowe
> If her white necke be shadowde with blacke haire,
> Whey so was *Ledas*, yet was *Leda* faire.
> Amber trest is shee, then on the morne thinke I,
> My love alludes to everie historie:
> A yong wench pleaseth, and an old is good,
> This for her looks, that for her woman-hood:
> Now what is she that any Romane loves,
> But my ambitious ranging mind approves?

The happy Englishing of *est etiam in fusco grata colore Venus*
by "nut-brown girles in doing hath no fellowe," and the
Marlovian "ambitious ranging mind," have been admired before
now.[6]

In contrast to this delight that the poet can love all women,
the ninth poem in Marlowe's selection, 3.6, shows us the poet
unable to make love to any woman at all: "Yet like as if cold
hemlocke I had drunke, / It mocked me, hung down the head
and suncke." Yet even in this plight the poet remembers, if only
for the sake of contrast, the variety of his former loves:

> Yet boorded I the golden *Chie* twise,
> And *Libas*, and the white cheek'de *Pitho* thrise,
> *Corinna* cravde it in a summers night,
> And nine sweete bouts had we before day light.

Between these two poems, the one full of sexual success, the other of sexual failure, comes 2.10, a poem which begins with a sexual dilemma:

> *Graecinus* (well I wot) thou touldst me once,
> I could not be in love with twoo at once,
> By thee deceived, by thee surprisde am I,
> For now I love two women equalie.

The dilemma is soon resolved. The poet will simply abandon the notion of confining his attentions to one woman: "Let one wench cloy me with sweete loves delight, / If one can doote, if not, two everie night." He is *capable de tout*:

> Pleasure addes fuell to my lustful fire,
> I pay them home with that they most desire:
> Oft have I spent the night in wantonnesse,
> And in the morne been lively neverethelesse.

Thus 2.4, 2.10, and 3.6 form a group treating the possibilities of promiscuity and contrasting with 1.3, 1.5, and 3.13, all of which proclaimed the poet's attachment to a single woman. We can now see the basic arrangement of Marlowe's selection:

1.1 The power of love
1.3 Fidelity: enthusiastic loyalty
1.5 (Fidelity): Corinna's divided mind
3.13 Fidelity: unwilling loyalty
1.15
1.13 The central poems
2.4 Promiscuity: enthusiastic potency
2.10 (Promiscuity): the poet's divided mind
3.6 Promiscuity: dejected impotence
1.2 The power of love

The first poem and the last are joined to the second and the penultimate by similarity or contrast of themes. In 1.1 the poet tells how the power of love made him write love-elegy instead of epic; in 1.3 the poet reminds Corinna of the power of poetry to confer immortality: "So likewise we will through the world by rung, / And with my name shall thine be alwaies sung." The last poem, 1.2, celebrates the triumphant omnipotence of Love and his victory over the poet; it follows 3.6, in which the poet defeated by love bewails his own impotence.

What of the two remaining poems, 1.15 and 1.13? Their position at the center of what is evidently a careful and symmetrical arrangement of poems suggests that they are in some way important to the collection, either as statements of some idea important to the arranger or as clues to further significance in the arrangement itself. We shall have to look, but first we shall have to consider how far we are entitled to look and how recondite our speculation may be allowed to become.

Once the fact of organization around a central feature has been established it seems that we may look very far indeed. Alastair Fowler has shown how important the "central feature" is in Elizabethan poetry, especially poetry having a triumph as part of its design. The center was the place for kings:

> An outstanding feature of triumphal motifs is their emphasis of the centre. This position once carried a generally recognized iconological significance: it was the place, if not for an image of sovereignty, at least for a 'central feature' (to use an idiom still current). The sovereign might occupy either the centre of a circle, such as the zodiacal border of an imperial coin, or the mid point of a linear array, as when a throne was placed at the centre of one side of a table. In the linear form, elaborate symmetries often surround the significant middle point.[7]

Renaissance poets were willing to go to great lengths to incorporate this emphasis on centrality into the design of their poems, and they reinforced or ornamented their design with allusion to extra-poetic symmetries. In Spenser's *Epithalamion* symmetrical organization of stanzas in triads and tetrads around the two stanzas (12 and 13) describing the wedding ceremony combines with an elaborate system of allusion to astronomical events so that the poem itself becomes a kind of orrery replicating the cosmic circumstances of the poet's wedding day. There are—to name only the most obvious referents—24 stanzas, 365 long lines, and 16 stanzas with positive refrain and 8 with negative refrain, corresponding to the 16 hours of daylight and 8 of night on the day Spenser was married.[8]

Guided by these considerations and having our search authorized by the obvious symmetrical arrangement of the ten poems thus: 1 3 2 3 1, we may begin to look for the center of Marlowe's selection. Cupid's triumph (1.2), for the last poem, is another clue. By wrenching it from the place Ovid gave it, Marlowe calls our attention to triumphs and reminds us of the Renaissance convention that at the center of the triumph was the sovereign triumphant, and by placing 1.15, the last poem of the first book of the *Amores*, in the fifth place at the center of his collection of ten poems, he confirms this emphasis. Near the end of 1.15 occur kings and triumphs: "Let Kings give place to verse, and kingly shows, / And banks ore which gold bearing *Tagus* flowes." Ovid is more explicit: *cedant carminibus reges regumque triumphi, / cedat et auriferi ripa benigna Tagi.* These lines were even nearer the end in the poem as it appeared in Mirandula's *Flores Poetarum*, where most Renaissance readers saw it. That version ended with the next couplet, which Shakespeare chose as the motto for *Venus and Adonis: vilia miretur vulgus; mihi flavus Apollo / pocula castalia plena ministret aqua.* At the center (vv. 9–30 of 42) of *Amores* 1.15, which expounds the proposition "Verse is immortall, and shall nere decay," is another kind of triumph; twelve poets, six Greek and six Roman, parade before us. The device was used again by Ben Jonson in his "To the memory of my beloved. . .Mr. William Shakespeare." Six English authors (Chaucer, Spenser, Beaumont; Lyly, Kyd, Marlowe) and six ancient authors (Aeschylus, Euripides, Sophocles; Pacuvius, Accius, Seneca) precede the central lines (41–42 of 80), "Triumph, my Britaine, thou hast one to showe, / To whom all Scenes of Europe homage owe."[9]

Marlowe, then, arranged his selection from Ovid in such a way that its extremities would direct us to its central feature, the triumph of poetry over kings and kingly shows. Although he is weak and helpless before triumphant Love, the poet himself has a power beyond any of society's powers; his verse can confer immortality. By placing the triumph of poetry fifth in his selection, Marlowe enables his readers to draw on Renaissance numerological doctrine to strengthen the triumphal sovereignty of poetry. Five was the number of sovereignty:

> To enlarge this contemplation unto all the mysteries and secrets, accomodable unto this number, were inexcusable Pythagorisme, yet cannot omit the ancient conceit of five surnamed the number of justice; as justly dividing between the digits, and hanging in the centre of Nine, described by square numeration, which angularly divided will make the decussated number; and so agreeable unto the Quincunciall Ordination, and rowes divided by Equality, and just *Decorum*, in the whole com-plantation; And might be the Originall of that common game among us, wherein the fifth place is Soveraigne, and carrieth the chief intention.[10]

Here Sir Thomas Browne thinks of five as the central position in the Pythagorean square number nine; that is, "three squared" or three rows of three, in the center of which hangs the fifth position.[11] Taking our cue from him, we may ask what significance a Renaissance reader well versed in Pythagorism might have found in the number ten, the total of poems in Marlowe's selection.

Ten, called the Tetractys of the Decad, is equal to the sum of consecutive integers beginning with one $(1 + 2 + 3 + 4 = 10)$. The Pythagoreans held that number, far from being a simple ordering device, was capable of extension into space, and that in fact all dimensions could be understood in terms of number. Thus the monad, one, represented a point; extended into space as the dyad, two, it became a line; further extension produced the triad, three, a plane surface; finally, with extension to the tetrad, four, a solid appeared. Since all dimensional possibilities are thus exhausted, the decad, $1 + 2 + 3 + 4$, contains all possible forms of number, and since number is the basis of reality, ten represents in its perfection all of creation: "As the number 10 is thought to be perfect and to comprise the whole nature of numbers, they [sc., the Pythagoreans] say that the bodies which move through the heavens are ten, but as the visible bodies are only nine, to meet this they invent a tenth—the 'counter-earth.'"[12]

Petrus Bongus, a Renaissance numerologist, gives additional reasons for the special perfection of ten. It contains every kind of number: even, like two; odd, like three; and those made of even and odd, like five (2 + 3). Because the Arabic numerals are ten in number, ten can be said to contain *cunctos singulatim numeros.* In counting we begin to re-use the numerals once ten has been reached; it is therefore a circular number and sums up in the return to unity all natural processes: the return of water to the sea, the body to the earth, the soul to God. In considering the significance of the number ten for Marlowe's selection from Ovid, however, our concern must be with a subsidiary aspect of the decad's perfection and summation of the universe. Here Bongus will provide our starting point.

> So it happens that in the Decad, written thusly: 10, may be seen a clear image of man's rational frame. For just as the Decad is compounded of Unity, 1, and the character for emptiness, so human existence consists of soul and body. Human intellect is an intellect not of itself, but rather an intellect clothed in the otherness of the body; the body, moreover, does not keep the soul in place of its own being. Therefore the way of writing Unity expresses the mind of man, but the joining to it of otherness and emptiness expresses the appearance of the human body.*

The passage is interesting not least for its illustration of how far Renaissance numerologists were willing to carry their search for significance in number and how readily they adapted to their system new developments in mathematics—in this case, the use of zero. Because ten is written by joining the numerals one, the monad or unity, and zero, the "otherwhere" (*alteritas*) of number

---

* Quo fit, ut in Denario qui ad hunc modum pingitur 10: manifesta Rationalis fabricae conspiciatur imago. Quemadmodum enim Denarius ex Unitate, & privationis forma conflatur: ita humana substantia animo, corporeque constat. Humanus intellectus est quidem intellectus, non tamen per se, sed intellectus inditus alteritati corporis. corpus autem ad animum, vicem non entis obtinet. Unitatis igitur character hominis exprimit animum; sed alteritatis & privationis appositio speciem gerit humani corporis (*Mysticae Numerorum Significatio,* Bergamo, 1585, part 2, p. 5).

that reveals only the fact that value is lacking, ten can be seen as a representation of the human intellect, in which pure mind, *animus*, unity, is joined with the body, lack of mind, zero.

The interpretation may seem farfetched, but in associating ten with the intellect Bongus was drawing on a well-known association in Renaissance thought. Ten represented all creation and all creative processes in the universe. By analogy of the macrocosm with the microcosm, therefore, it represented also human creativity. It was fitting, then, that ten should be the number of the nine Muses plus Apollo. When Spenser built the *Teares of the Muses* from ten complaints, he expected his readers to recognize the number as appropriate and to make the association of the poet with Apollo, the tenth member of the Muses' choir. To make up the cosmic number one hundred, each complaint has ten stanzas, with the exception of the poet's, which has nine, and Euterpe's, the fifth, which has eleven in compensation. The choir of ten, the Muses under Apollo's direction, was a conventional symbol of the cosmic harmony of nine spheres (earth, seven planets, and fixed stars) under the direction of the mind of God as well as for human creation directed by the mind of the artist. Marsilio Ficino is merely reflecting Plotinus when he reports that the Pythagoreans identified Apollo with cosmic harmony because his name represented Unity.[13]

Thus ten was an appropriate number for a selection designed to emphasize through symmetry and centrality of arrangement the primacy of poetry. In the center of Marlowe's selection, instead of kings we have the poet triumphant and the choir of ten:

> Let Kings give place to verse, and kingly showes,
> And banks ore which gold bearing *Tagus* flowes.
> Let base conceited wits admire vilde things,
> Faire *Phoebus* lead me to the Muses springs.
> About my head be quivering Mirtle wound,
> And in sad lovers heads let me be found.

This central emphasis on the sovereignty of poetry and on the poet's special closeness to Apollo and the Muses combines two Renaissance conventions—the association of five and the center with sovereignty, and the association of ten with Apollo and the

Muses, cosmic creativity, and poetry—to confirm a theme stressed at beginning and end of the selection. In 1.1 the poet, compelled by Love, rejected public poetry, epic, in favor of love elegy. In 1.3 the poet reminded his mistress of the power of poetry to grant immortality and argued that a poet's standing was as good as a nobleman's:

> If loftie titles cannot make me thine,
> That am descended but of knightly line,
> Soone may you plow the little lands I have,
> I gladly graunt my parents given to save,
> *Apollo*, *Bacchus*, and the Muses say,
> And *Cupide* who hath markt me for thy pray.

In 1.2, the last poem in the selection, a public motif, the triumph, became an image for the power of Love and, by extension, of love-poetry. The final triumph also alerted us, in accordance with Renaissance conventions of arrangement, to look for symmetrical arrangement and a central, sovereign feature.

But, it may be objected, Sir Thomas Browne spoke of five as being sovereign in the midst of nine, not ten, and the fifth poem, even the end of the fifth poem, is not strictly speaking the center of a series of ten. Renaissance numerology, however, did not always see ten as a linear number. Ten was also a triangular number, part of a familiar series "including the perfect numbers 6 and 28, the expanded form of the *tetractys* 10, the 'great quaternion' 36 and the number of complete life 120."[14] If we arrange the ten poems of Marlowe's selection as a triangle, the centrality of 1.15 becomes evident:

```
              1.1
           1.3   1.5
       3.13   1.15   1.13
   2.4   2.10   3.6   1.2
```

A Renaissance reader accustomed to visualize numbers as two-dimensional arrays as well as simple series and to examine the symbolic associations of such arrays would have had no difficulty in seeing the ten poems in this way. The triangular arrangement, moreover, was especially appropriate to a selection whose central poem treated the power of poetry to confer immortality and the superiority of poetry to kingly shows. The two ideas had been linked with triangular structures ever since Horace: *Exegi monumentum aere perennius / regalique situ pyramidum altius*.[15] The triangular form of ten in particular evoked not only the immortality of poetry but also the fourfold (1 + 2 + 3 + 4) universe as a whole and the threefold principle of creativity manifest in macrocosm and microcosm, in Apollo with his Muses and in the poet.

The symmetrical arrangement (1 3 2 3 1) of poems that caught our attention earlier directed us to not one but two central poems, 1.15 and 1.13. What of the latter? Why did Marlowe include it in his selection? His rendering of the famous aubade is, first of all, a delightful translation of an equally delightful poem. Marlowe liked Ovid's poem well enough to have Faustus quote from it—inappropriately, some might say—as he is about to be taken away to Hell, and J. B. Steane, after quoting Marlowe's version entire, sums up by saying, "The poet who can translate like this, whose feeling for verse-movement (for instance) can produce lines as sensitive as the first couplet, does not need our indulgence; but his works might as well be buried with him if they do not secure and promote our delight."[16]

But *Amores* 1.13 has also a place in the scheme of arrangement that we have noticed in Marlowe's selection from the *Amores*. If we follow Renaissance practice and look for the central lines of the selection, we discover that the central couplet, 224 lines from the beginning of the 448-line selection, is "*Jove* that thou shouldst not hast but wait his leasure, / Made two nights one to finish up his pleasure." Ovid here refers to the story of how Jove, in order to give himself more time for making love to Alcmena, doubled the length of their night together.

The arranger's wit is subtle and suggestive. The center was the place for triumphant sovereigns, and in 1.15 the central emphasis of the selection fell on the poet associated with Apollo and triumphant over kings and kingly shows. It was also the place for the sun; indeed, the association of sun and sovereign far antedates the Renaissance.[17] In the Ptolemaic system the sun occupied the middle sphere of the seven planetary spheres as one moved away from the central earth.[18] Cartari's influential handbook associates the sun's place in the universe with Apollo's central place among the Muses:

> The sunne standeth amidst the planets, commanding them to hasten or enslacke their revolutions, in manner as in efficient vigor and strength they receive from him their vertues and operations. And for this cause likewise the auncients called him the head or guide of the Muses.[19]

It is therefore entirely appropriate that at the second, less evident center of Marlowe's selection there should be a reference to the king of the gods, and that, just as Jove delayed the coming of the sun by making night twice its normal length, so the arranger has placed two poems, not one, at the center of his selection and postponed the actual center by line count until after the structural center, which came at the end of 1.15.

This fitness extends to other aspects of the second central poem. By placing Ovid's aubade here, Marlowe strengthens implications of the poem's hypothesis which are left unstressed by Ovid. The symmetrical arrangement of poems around 1.15 and 1.13 revealed the poet in 1.15 triumphant over the powers of this earth and even, through his power to immortalize in verse, over death. The placing of 1.13 where it is suggests that the poet's powers may go even farther.

In isolation—and in Ovid—the aubade is merely a witty conceit, an effective way for the poet to say that he doesn't want to get up from his lover's side now that morning has come. But the analogy of his creative intellect with the divine creative intellect identified the Renaissance poet with Apollo, leader of the Muses' choir, with the sun, and with the intellectual force that set the universe in motion. The Renaissance artist was to be a magus who by imitating nature would control it. By placing Ovid's aubade sixth in his selection of ten translations, after the central emphasis on the power of poetry and the association of the poet with Apollo, Marlowe transforms the poet's request to the dawn from a mere conceit into a command that might be obeyed.

Day comes, all the same: "I chid no more, she blusht, and therefore heard me, / Yet lingered not the day, but morning scard me." The artist-magus's command is not obeyed, any more than

Faustus's *lente, lente currite noctis equi* from the same poem. But the Dawn does hear, for she blushes red. In Ovid this characteristic ironical coda revealed the poet saving face by projectng his own egotistical desires onto the unchangeable natural world. The reddening dawn showed up the emptiness of the poet's mythological conceit. In Marlowe the Dawn's blushes confirm the poet's power. Has he not, after all, delayed the dawn-*poem* until after the center of his pyramid of poetry, where we would on one scheme of reckoning expect the sun to be? And has he not delayed also the real, mathematical center of his selection, the central couplet with its reference to Jove's delaying the sun, until after the structural center of the selection at the end of 1.15 and beginning of 1.13?

The poet's special immortality claimed in 1.15, in fact, is the basis of his claimed ability to control the sun in 1.13, for his identification with Apollo is, as we have seen, also an identification with the sun. One of Marlowe's manipulations of Ovid shows him highlighting this identification and links the end of one central poem with the beginning of the other. At the end of 1.15, Ovid writes *ergo etiam cum me supremus adederit ignis, / vivam, parsque mei multa superstes erit.* Marlowe renders this couplet by "Then though death rackes my bones in funerall fier, / Ile live, and as he puls me down, mount higher." (Again we note the echo of Faustus's situation.) Ovid's pentameter is literally "I'll live, and a great part of me will survive." By creating the image of the poet rising up in the flames of death, Marlowe suggests that the poet, who has just been crowned in triumph by the sun-god Apollo, imitates the sun which, in the next couplet at the beginning of 1.13, rises up behind the dawn: "Now on the sea from her old love comes shee, / That drawes the day from heavens cold axletree." The poet, magus-fashion, imitates that which he wishes to control. His victory over death is victory over the processes of the universe.

Nothing that I have said so far about Marlowe's translation of the *Amores* will, I think, alter the standard judgment on individual poems. Marlowe's successes and failures in rendering individual lines and poems remain what other scholars have noted them to be. But I hope that I have said enough to indicate what a disservice we do these translations when we read them in isolation. As line-for-line versions in heroic couplets they are unique, both against the background of earlier Ovids and in the corpus of Marlowe's works. Precisely because of this uniqueness they must be seen as a whole and assessed in their relation both to other translations and to the Renaissance world view out of which they grew and through which they should be read. Only thus can a true appreciation be formed of Marlowe's achievement in these translations.

Seen in this way, the Ovid translations do not succeed, but their failure dazzles. Marlowe's decision to proceed line by line, which may have been due to his recognition of numerological possibilities in a carefully arranged selection from the *Amores*, was fatal to his poetic success. This decision forced him to confine his attention to the single line and the single couplet. In the absence of a tradition of original composition in iambic pentameter couplets that might have shown him how to link couplets into longer units, as Ovid does, Marlowe produced a translation that reads as it was written, in single lines. And the quality of these single lines varies enormously. Finally, in fact, it is Marlowe's failure to be consistent, to strike a consistent tone and achieve a consistent level of poetic success in couplet after couplet, that makes the Ovid translations his least readable work.

Against these defects may be put two achievements. Marlowe is the first to recognize particular qualities of style in individual lines of Ovid and to attempt to reproduce these qualities in his English translation. By making his translation read like a translation, he exploits Renaissance conventions of reading to compel our attention toward his role as a shaper of the translation before us. Further, Marlowe is unique in his reordering of the original poems so as to intensify themes found in the original collection. All translation is criticism, and Marlowe's criticism of Ovid is to be discovered not only in the evaluation of Ovid's style implicit in Marlowe's choice—indeed, creation—of the terse and balanced measure for his translation, but also in his use of numerological doctrine and conventions of arrangement to point up themes that were important to him: the poet's special immortality, his superiority to "base conceited wits," and the power of his "ambitious ranging mind" to control nature by imitating it. If these achievements seem negligible because they force us to take account of external referents—the text of Ovid, or Renaissance numerology—it is perhaps as much as a fault of the way we read translations as of the way Marlowe made them.

3

George Sandys
A Translator between Two Worlds

In 1623, on a tiny ship crossing the Atlantic "amongst the roreing of the seas, the rustling of the Shroude, and the clamour of the Saylers," George Sandys, newly appointed treasurer of the Virginia Company, sat down to translate two books of Ovid's *Metamorphoses*.[1] Later, in the midst of the distractions of government in the New World, he translated eight more. In 1626, soon after he returned from America, a small folio appeared containing his version of all fifteen books. The reading public, whose appetite had been whetted by the publication of the first five books in 1621, praised the 1626 translation enthusiastically, and in 1632 Sandys issued a second, enlarged edition.[2] This edition, which is the one most people have in mind when they refer to "Sandys's Ovid," differs from its predecessor chiefly in the addition of some prefatory material, engraved plates before each book, and elaborate commentaries after. The translation itself received only minor modifications.[3]

Yet people are right to insist instinctively that the 1632 edition alone is to be called "Sandys's Ovid." The commentaries take up as much room as the translation, interpose themselves between books, and demand the reader's attention. On the commentaries is based the conventional judgment on Sandys's place in the prolonged collapse of the medieval world view that we call the Renaissance. According to this judgment Sandys's place is little, if at all, in advance of Golding's. "In certain respects Sandys in his 1632 edition is the last great representative of the tradition of allegorized interpretation which began in the Middle Ages."[4]

Or with less qualification:

> His commentary becomes . . . a convincing illustration of
> how sharply the medieval tradition had etched itself into
> the consciousness of the men of the late Renaissance. The
> spirit of the anonymous redactor of the *Ovide moralisé*
> lives on in George Sandys.
>
> But the commentary of Sandys was strictly an Indian
> summer flowering of the allegorical tradition, which in
> England and elsewhere was doomed to disappear. The
> forces which were eventually to destroy it had been
> gathering strength ever since the turn of the century.[5]

In this chapter I shall examine Sandys's use of Francis Bacon's
mythology and his relation to some of the changes in Ovid's
reputation which were taking place in his day. By so doing I hope
to show that the qualification "in certain respects" is necessary
to the truth of the first statement, and that the second view is
altogether overstated. For while it is true that much in Sandys's
commentary is drawn directly from the Ovid commentaries of
Sabinus and Raphael Regius or from mythological handbooks like
that of Natalis Comes, it is equally true that in several respects
Sandys belongs to his own age more than to any other. Super-
ficially, references to "*Galileos* Glasses" or stories with an
American setting, like that of the man saved from a rattlesnake
by the warning of a tame lizard, place the book in the early age
of modern science and English colonization of North America.[6]
On a deeper level, Sandy's view of ancient myth, although
it draws on many commonplaces of medieval and early Renais-
sance thought, cannot be wholly derived from them. Sandys
formed his ideas on the historical origin and truth value of myths
under the influence of Francis Bacon's writings. Recent scholar-
ship has rightly drawn attention to the traditional elements in
Bacon's thought,[7] but it remains true that the later seventeenth
century, with some justice, saw Bacon as the first of a new way
of thinking rather than the last of the old. Sandys cannot be called
the first modern translator any more than Bacon can be called
the first modern scientist, but equally he cannot be called the last
medieval allegorizer. Not only his Baconian view of myth, but
also, as we shall see, the place of his Ovid in the literary revalua-

tion begun by George Chapman of the Ovidian manner, forbid so simple an estimate of Sandys.

In fact, the phrase that Eduard Frankel used so well to describe Ovid may be applied equally to Sandys: he is a poet between two worlds. Ovid sat, sometimes uneasily, between republican and imperial Rome, between a literature of politics and a literature of rhetoric, between, in Frankel's view, pagan Rome and Christian Rome. Sandys likewise belongs neither wholly to the Renaissance nor to modern times; his conceptual world embraces witches and Galileo. Neither Ovid nor Sandys would have endorsed this description of their Janus-faces. We write from what we know, and we cannot know the future or read its books. But Sandys did, as it happened, sense that his Ovid belonged between two worlds. He is speaking of the geographical circumstances of its writing, but his words may apply as well to its spiritual location: "It needeth more than a single denization, being a double Stranger: Sprung from the Stocke of the ancient Romanes; but bred in the New-World, of the rudenesse whereof it cannot but participate; especially having Warres and Tumults to bring it to light, in stead of the Muses."[8]

Sandys and Bacon's Mythology

On an empty page ("so left," as he tells us, "by the oversight of the Printer") between his translation of Book 1 and his commentary on it, Sandys sees fits to mention the "principall Authors" out of whom he has compiled his commentaries. He names twenty-six: nine Greek (Plato, Palaephatus, Apollodorus, Aratus, Strabo, Diodorus, Pausanias, Plutarch, and Lucian); four Roman (Cicero, Hyginus, Pliny, and Macrobius); four church fathers (Lactantius, Eusebius, Augustine, and Fulgentius); and nine moderns (Geraldus, Pontanus, Ficinus, Vives, Comes, Scaliger, Sabinus, Pierius, "and the *Crowne of the latter*, the Viscount of St. Albons").[9] Francis Bacon died in the year in which the first edition without commentary of Sandys's complete translation was published. All Bacon's published works were available to the commentator; what did he owe to the author with whom he crowned his list of sources?

On one level the debt is obvious. We would not need Sandys's specific citation of Bacon at the beginning of this passage on the River Styx from the commentary on Book 2 to tell us how much it draws from Bacon's interpretation in chapter 5 of *De Sapientia Veterum*.[10]

But perhaps more accurately by the Viscount of *Saint Albons*: how leagues betweene Princes, though confirmed by oath, together with the bonds of merit, nature, or aliance, are commonly no longer of validity then they stand with the Reasons of state, and peculiar utility. Onely the obligation of necessity (represented by *Styx*, that fatall and unrepassable river) abideth firme and unviolable.

Fabula de foederibus et pactis principum conficta videtur: in quibus illud nimio plus quam oporteret verum est, foedera quacumque solemnitate et religione iuramenti parum firma esse; adeo ut fere ad existimationem quandam et famam et ceremoniam, magis quam ad fidem et securitatem et effectum adhibeantur. Itaque unum assumitur verum et proprium fidei firmamentum, neque illud divinitas aliqua coelestis: ea est Necessitas ...Necessitas autem per Stygem eleganter repraesentatur, flumen fatale et irremeabile.

No fewer than seventeen of Sandys's interpretations of myth come in this way directly from Bacon.[11]

Differences, omissions, and additions may be as illuminating as similarities. In the preceding paragraph I have quoted more than half of Bacon's interpretation. All of it is directed toward explaining how the myth of the River Styx represents the truth about treaties and leagues between princes. But Sandys, although he allows that Bacon's interpretation is perhaps nearer the heart of the myth than others, presents it as only one in a series of interpretations and comments. That the pagan gods swore by the river of Hell argues their mortality, as Lactantius says. The Styx is a river in Arcadia, and its water is so corrosive a poison that nothing can contain it but a mule's hoof. Perhaps it acquires its poisonous character from some such subterranean exhalation as Sandys himself saw, "in a dry and lightsome cave betweene *Naples* and *Putzoll,* to kill a dog in as short a time as I am in telling of it." The name "Styx" means "sorrow," says Regius. There is a story that Styx sent her daughter Victory to aid the gods in their war with the giants; in return for this assistance, Jupiter granted Styx the privilege that whoever swore falsely by her name should be banished from the festivals and councils of the gods. Aristotle says that this myth signifies that water is the first and most ancient element, for nothing is to be preferred to the sanctity of an oath. Only after all this commentary and more do we come to Sandys's presentation of Bacon's interpretation.

Sandys condenses Bacon's explication, and his selection from it reveals that he was no mere recorder of another man's opinions. He tones down Bacon's Machiavellianism and is altogether less skeptical of the sanctity of a prince's oath. Bacon says that princes' promises are not, unfortunately, to be depended on, no matter what the solemn oaths by which they are bound: *illud nimio plus quam oporteret verum est, foedera quacumque solemnitate et religione iuramenti munita parum firma esse.* These promises are commonly undertaken only to advance the prince's reputation and not from considerations of honesty, security, or effect: *adeo ut fere ad existimationem quandam et famam et ceremoniam, magis quam ad fidem et securitatem et effectum adhibentur.* Further, even ties of kinship, which are Nature's sacraments, or mutual good services are rated by many below ambition, utility, and unbridled exercise of power: *Quin si accesserint etiam affinitatis vincla, veluti Sacramenta Naturae, si merita mutua, tamen omnia infra ambitionem et utilitatem et dominationis licentiam esse apud plerosque reperiuntur.* The words of princes, in fact, cannot be trusted; since they are accountable to no one, they can always find some pretext to mask their bad faith: *Tanto magis, quod principibus facile sit per praetextus varios et speciosos cupiditates suas et fidem minus sinceram (nemine rerum arbitro, cui ratio sit reddenda) tueri et velare.*

Sandys omits this last damning suggestion altogether. He will not allow a prince to break an oath from *ambitio,* and Bacon's *dominationis licentiam* becomes "Reasons of state"—which is hardly the same thing. Sandys compresses the rest of Bacon's indictment of princes' reliability into a single concessive clause, omitting as he does the uncomplimentary suggestion that princes in taking oaths look more to their reputation than to the demands of honesty, and transforms the vigorous metaphor in *solemnitate et religione iuramenti munita* into "confirmed by oath."

"Leagues betweene Princes, though confirmed by oath, together with the bonds of merit, nature, or aliance, are commonly no longer of validity then they stand with the Reasons of state, and peculiar utility." Sandys has not, in fact, given us Bacon's interpretation but instead a muted and dignified transformation of it. He enjoyed and expected the patronage of royalty, but even though a desire to avoid offending his patron may account for his handling of Bacon's remarks on the perfidy of princes, we must still ask what implications there are in the fact of the transformation. Sandys has not merely condensed; he has selected and criticized. If Bacon is consistent in his interpretation of the myth, Sandys is equally consistent in the drift of his reworking of Bacon. Seeing what Sandys admired in the Viscount St. Albans's mythology may help us to understand why he undertook the translation of Ovid.

References to ancient myths appear throughout Bacon's works. For him, as for every other educated man of his time, the old stories were part of the mind's furniture, there to be used if required as readily as modern or ancient history, and in the same way:

> For let a man look into the errors of Clement the seventh,
> so lively described by Guiciardine, who served under
> him, or into the errors of Cicero painted out by his own
> pencil in his Epistles to Atticus, and he will fly apace from
> being irresolute. Let him look into the errors of Phocion,
> and he will beware how he be obstinate or inflexible. Let
> him but read the fable of Ixion, and it will hold him from
> being vaporous or imaginative.[12]

Bacon, as we might expect, uses myth for more than mere decoration of ideas; in fact, he explicitly condemns the indiscriminate exploitation of myth by those who are more concerned with manufacturing support for their own ideas than with discovering the truths conveyed by the myths:

> Not but that I know very well what pliant stuff fable is
> made of, how freely it will follow any way you please
> to draw it, and how easily with a little dexterity and
> discourse of wit meanings which it was never meant to
> bear may be plausibly put upon it . . . that many, wishing
> only to gain the sanction and reverence of antiquity for
> doctrines and inventions of their own, have tried to twist
> the fables of the poets into that sense; that this is neither
> a modern vanity nor a rare one, but old of standing and
> frequent in use.*

The quest for the truths behind the myths occupied Bacon
at intervals throughout his life, especially in his fifth decade and
again shortly before he died.[13] The study of mythology was a
quest, not an idle pastime. Bacon would have dismissed as worse
than idle Cervantes's "humanist," whose classical learning had
produced a book of "seven hundred and three devices with their
colours, mottoes and ciphers," from which "gentlemen of the
court could extract and use whatever they pleased at festival time
and celebrations, and would then have no need to beg their
liveries from anybody, or to rack their brains, as they say, to
invent them to suit their desires and purposes."[14] Behind the
ancient myths lay truth which the stories themselves had been
designed to convey and conceal.

Bacon never abandoned his belief that the myths whose
purpose it was to conceal truth had been formulated after the
truths they concealed; he did, however, assert it with varying
degrees of conviction.[15] In a frequently quoted passage from *The
Advancement of Learning*, Bacon says,

> I do rather think that the fable was first, and the
> exposition devised, than that the moral was first, and
> thereupon the fable formed.[16]

---

* Neque me latet quam versatilis materia sit fabula, ut huc illuc trahi, imo et duci
possit; quantumque ingenii commoditas et discursus valeat, ut quae numquam
cogitata sint belle tamen attribuantur . . . multi enim, ut inventis et placitis
suis antiquitatis venerationem acquirerent, poetarum fabulas ad ea traducere
conati sunt. Atque vetus illa vanitas et frequens, neque nuper nata, aut raro
usurpata est (*De Sapientia Veterum* praef. = *Works* 6:626).

The context makes it clear that he is not talking about all myths but only some literary manifestations of them. He condemns Chrysippus for his attempt to fasten Stoic doctrine onto ancient poetry, then continues,

> But yet that all the fables and fictions of the poets were but pleasure and not figure, I interpose no opinion. Surely of those poets which are now extant, even Homer himself (notwithstanding he was made a kind of Scripture by the later schools of the Grecians), yet I should without any difficulty pronounce that his fables had no such inwardness in his own meaning; but what they might have upon a more original tradition, is not easy to affirm; for he was not the inventor of many of them.

The reference to Chrysippus redirects us to the preface of the *De Sapientia Veterum*, where Bacon again uses him, along with the alchemical allegorizers, as an example of tendentious interpretation.

> Chrysippus long ago, interpreting the oldest poets after the manner of an interpreter of dreams, made them out to be Stoics.... [T]he Alchemists more absurdly still have discovered in the pleasant and sportive fictions of the transformation of bodies, allusions to experiments of the furnace.*

The existence of these frivolous and wrong-headed interpretations does not detract from the honor due to myths, for some of them contain truths from the beginning.

> I do certainly for my own part (I freely and candidly confess) incline to this opinion,—that beneath no small number of the fables of the ancient poets there lay from the very beginning a mystery and an allegory.†

---

* Nam et olim Chrysippus Stoicorum opiniones vetustissimis poetis, veluti somniorum aliquis interpres, ascribere solebat; et magis insulse Chymici ludos et delicias poetrarum in corporum transformationibus ad fornacis experimenta transtulerunt.

† Fateor certe ingenue et libenter, me in hanc sententiam propendere, ut non paucis antiquorum poetarum fabulis mysterium et allegoriam iam ab origine subesse putem.

Perhaps because we are misled by the fact that the conflict between ancients and moderns in the later seventeenth century was a conflict between emerging modern thought and the classical antiquity we know, it is easy for us to forget that the *veteres* of *De Sapientia Veterum* are not, in fact, Virgil, Plato, or even Homer. Chrysippus interpreting Homer was in Bacon's view a mere *somniorum interpres*, an interpreter of dreams. If Chrysippus is an *interpres*, then the fables of Homer are no more than *somnia*. "He was not the inventor of many of them." There is, of course, truth in dreams, as well as much that is false or irretrievably lost in confusion. Bacon believed that many of the myths had originated in a period after the Fall but before the earliest Greek thinkers. The ancient wise men of this time had set down as myths their insights into the true nature of the world. Later, when men began to study words and not things, the truth of these insights was lost.[17]

By studying the myths and discovering the truths in them, Bacon hoped to recover something of the power that man had held over nature before the Fall. The source of this power, an eloquent passage from the *Valerius Terminus* suggests, is language:

> And therefore it is not the pleasure of curiosity, nor the quiet of resolution, nor the raising of the spirit, nor victory of wit, nor faculty of speech, nor lucre of profession, nor ambition of honour or fame, nor inablement for business, that are the true ends of knowledge; some of these being more worthy than other, though all inferior and degenerate: but it is a restitution and reinvesting (in great part) of man to the sovereignty and power (for whensoever he shall be able to call the creatures by their true names he shall again command them) which he had in his first state of creation.[18]

Adam's naming of the animals was a perfect matching of Word and World. The recovery, so far as possible, of this "commerce between the mind of man and the nature of things"[19] that existed before the Fall will give man power over the World through his understanding of the Word. Adam gave the animals names that were in perfect accord with their natures; they were, essentially and absolutely, what he called them. From the moment of his creation he knew the world, and because he knew it he could speak and command it. If we can recover Adam's words from the myths of the ancients, we too can command the world. Only God's name is secret and ineffable.[20]

These are deep and dangerous waters. A course can be plotted across them leading in one direction to the Royal Society and its search for a real character and universal language, and in the other to Hermeticism, Neoplatonism, and the Renaissance magi. Further, understanding Bacon's almost mystic idea of language as a necessary means of knowing and using the power of truth makes it easy to understand how his scientific method cannot be separated from his rhetoric and dialectic.[21] But we must return to Sandys, and to an illustration of the way in which Bacon's mythology affected not only the translator's interpretations of and comments on specific myths but also his explicit statement of the meaning of his work.

Opposite the frontispiece to the 1632 edition of *Ovid's Metamorphosis* Sandys placed an explanation in verse, "The Minde of the Frontispiece, and Argument of this Worke." The explanation proper, in large type, is both conventional and sweeping and does not altogether succeed in avoiding confusion of the physical and moral interpretations of myth. This confusion reveals Bacon's influence on the 1632 *Metamorphosis*. According to Sandys, Love, uniting the four elements, creates out of Chaos the harmony of Nature, "who, with ravisht eye, / Affects his owne-made *Beauties*." I take this last somewhat confusing expression to mean that Love (who is masculine, as in Bacon's *De Sapientia Veterum*, chapter 17, despite the prominence of Venus in the frontispiece itself) causes an affect, or appetite, in the natural and harmonious world which he created. Sandys's enigmatic expression can be traced back to chapter 17 of *De Sapientia Veterum*, "Cupido, sive Atomus," where we find the same confusion of physical and moral interpretation of myth.[22]

In Bacon's interpretation of the myth of Cupid, the *Amor* of the fable is nothing less than the natural motion of the atom, the primal, unique force that fashions all things from matter. It has no parent, that is, no antecedent cause (God, of course, excepted).[23] This ultimate natural cause lies beyond the range of human inquiry; hence it is represented as having hatched from the egg of Night. Love is perpetually a child, because things compounded of the atomic seeds of matter are large in relation to them and suffer aging and decay, whereas the seeds themselves are both incomprehensibly small and perpetually unchanging, that is, young. Love is naked, because things compounded of atoms are clothed in attributes and qualities, but the atoms themselves have none of the features that clothe their compounds. Bacon's language is not altogether clear at this point. As often, he uses language that is itself metaphorical (*personata et induta, nudum*) to describe allegory, so that his interpretation amounts to a restatement of the myth.[24] His brief remarks in the *De Sapientia Veterum* must be read in the light of his extended treatment of the myth of Cupid in the *De Principiis atque Originibus secundum fabulas Cupidinis et Coeli*. There he uses Cupid's nakedness as the starting point for a refutation of the idea that secondary qualities can be assigned to primary matter.[25] Love is blind, because the motions of atoms are not governed by foresight but only be mechanistic cause and effect. Love is an archer, because the *virtus atomi* must act through the distances, however minute, between atoms.

It is when he turns to the younger Cupid, Venus's son, that Bacon falls into the confusion which is reflected in Sandys's "Minde of the Frontispiece." Bacon recognizes that in the person of this younger Cupid the allegory moves from natural to moral philosophy, from the Eros who reconciles cosmic strife to the Cupid who makes us fall in love, but his correlation of the two is unsatisfactory. Later he would maintain that each myth conveyed a truth either natural, political, or moral and would avoid mixing the three philosophies.[26] In chapter 17 of the *De Sapientia Veterum*, he attempts to reconcile the two Cupids by suggesting that the older, cosmic binding force and the younger, personal divinity who makes human beings fall in love are one and the same. The impulse to love one fellow creature as opposed to another comes from causes that, because they are obscure, resemble the *virtus atomi*, the older Cupid. From Venus comes the general disposition toward mating and procreation, and from her son comes the specific sympathy directing our affections to one particular person.

For Venus excites the general appetite of conjunction and procreation; Cupid, her son, applies the appetite to an individual object. From Venus therefore comes the general disposition, from Cupid the more exact sympathy. Now the general disposition depends upon causes near at hand, the particular sympathy upon principles more deep and fatal, and as if derived from that ancient Cupid, who is the source of all exquisite sympathy.*

But are the causes of the general, Venereal disposition nearer because they are always readier to hand, being more generally distributed than the specific, Erotic impulse, which may or may not be present in any individual? Or are they nearer because the general disposition from Venus in each person is somehow the immediate cause of love or affection for another, while the specific impulse from Eros acts farther up the chain of causation in ways that we cannot understand? No matter how we interpret such difficult phrases as *a causis magis propinquis* or *exquisita sympathia*, it is evident that Bacon's exposition here is far from lucid. *Subest tamen quaedam eius cum illo antiquo conformitas*, he says, speaking of the younger Cupid, and earlier *in quem* [sc., *iuniorem*] *antiquioris attributa transferuntur, et quodam modo competunt*. The hedging *quaedam* and *quodam modo* betray his uncertainty.

Bacon's confusion has left its mark in Sandys. The translator's swift movement from the four elements, harmonized from Chaos by Love, to the "*Will, Desire,* and *Powres Irascible*" of men, ordered by the skill of Pallas, takes place in the phrase isolated earlier, in which Love "with ravisht eye, / Affects his owne-made *Beauties.*" Sandys has not even attempted to separate the older, cosmic Cupid from the younger divinity who works in our hearts, and Bacon's suggestion of *quaedam conformitas* between them lies behind the compressed argumentation of the "Minde of the Frontispiece." Further, a trace of Bacon's description of the actions

---

* Venus enim generaliter affectum coniunctionis et procreationis excitat; Cupido eius filius affectum ad individuum applicat. Itaque a Venere est generalis dispositio, a Cupidine magis exacta sympathia; atque illa a causis magis propinquis pendet; haec autem a principiis magis altis et fatalibus, et tanquam ab antiquo illo Cupidine, a quo omnis exquisita sympathia pendet (*Works* 6:656–57).

of Venus and Cupid as an *affectum coniunctionis* and *affectum ad individuum* can be seen in Sandys's choice of the verb "affects."

The rest of the "Minde of the Frontispiece" continues in a conventional vein. Those who follow Pallas, "who the mind attires / With all *Heroick Vertues*," will aspire to fame and glory and gain immortality. Those "who forsake that fair *Intelligence*, / To follow *Passion*, and voluptuous *Sense*," will be as nearly beasts as Pallas's followers are nearly gods. The choice of Hercules is duly adduced. We should not expect detailed argumentation from what is after all only Sandy's brief guide to his frontispiece; still, we notice that the question that threw Bacon into confusion has, after receiving a characteristic moralizing tint from Sandys's brush, been left unanswered. What is the connection between macrocosm and microcosm, between "powerfull *Love*," on the one hand, which unites the four elements, and "*Passion*, and voluptuous *Sense*," on the other, which, if men follow it, reduces them to beasts? There is no answer in Sandys.

In smaller type below the explanation of the elements, Love, and Pallas, Sandys sets out the relation of the *Metamorphoses* to these truths:

Phoebus Apollo (sacred poesy)
Thus taught: for in these ancient Fables lie
The mysteries of all Philosophie.

Some Natures secrets shew; in some appeare
Distemperes staines; some teach us how to beare
Both Fortunes, bridling Joy, Griefe, Hope, and Feare.

These Pietie, Devotion those excite;
These prompt to Vertue, those from Vice affright;
All fitly minging [sic] Profit with Delight.

The premise is Baconian: "as hieroglyphics were before letters, so parables were before arguments." The myths convey truths whose discovery antedates any expression of them in antiquity; hence the ancient stories must be attributed to Phoebus Apollo, not to Ovid or any other ancient author.

A bit farther on in his address "To the Reader" Sandys elaborates on these ideas:

> ...in this second Edition of my Translation, I have attempted (with what successe I submit to the Reader) to collect out of sundrie Authors the Philosophicall sense of these fables of Ovid; if I may call them his, when most of them are more antient then any extant Author, or perhaps then Letters themselves; before which, as they expressed their Conceptions in Hieroglyphickes, so did they their Philosophie and Divinitie under Fables and Parables: a way not un-trod by the sacred Pen-men; as by the prudent Law-givers, in their reducing of the old World to civilitie, leaving behind a deeper impression, then can be made by the livelesse precepts of Philosophie.

In its assertion that myths originated in a time before the earliest extant remains of antiquity and in its belief that myths were designed to teach truths which would be difficult of access if expressed prosaically, this passage bears the print of Bacon's mythology.

Bacon believed that myth had a twofold function: to teach, so that "inventions that are new and abstruse and remote from vulgar opinions may find an easier passage to the understanding,"[27] and to conceal, "to disguise and veil the meaning." Sandys's implicit rejection of this second function forms one of the major differences between his approach to myth and Bacon's. Sandys sees himself as an educator, not a Baconian explorer after truth. Hence he concentrates on explicating myths whose purpose agrees with his own. He directs his work to a wide and not greatly learned public.

> I have also added Marginall notes for illustration and ease of the meere English Reader, since divers places in our Author are otherwise impossible to be understood but by those who are well versed in the ancient Poets and Historians; withall to avoid the confusion of names which are given to one person, derived from his Ancestors, Country, Quality, or Achievements.

By "meere English Reader" Sandys means not those who have no Latin at all but those for whom Latin is more a memory from school days than an everyday habit.

The educational tenor of Sandys's work accounts for his emphasis on the moral and political interpretation of myth at the expense of the physical or scientific. His belief that books should "informe the understanding, direct the will, and temper the affections" leads him to emphasize those aspects of myth interpretation that will most directly advance this purpose. Sandys does not, however, neglect physical interpretations of myth, especially in Book 1 where Ovid's account of the creation of the world demands such explanations. He is always ready to record natural phenomena that he has seen or heard from others; indeed, personal, anecdotal narrative plays a larger part in Sandys's commentary than in any earlier Renaissance Ovid, and this characteristic of the commentary reveals the influence of Bacon's emphasis on the value of collecting observations. An extended quotation will give the flavor of Sandys's treatment of natural phenomena. He is discussing *Metamorphoses* 1.32–35:

> What God soever this division wrought,
> And every part to due proportion brought;
> First, least the Earth unequall should appeare,
> He turn'd it round, in figure of a sphere.

Sandys comments that the earth is

> ...made round, that it might be equall in it selfe; and equally distant from the celestiall bodies, from whence it receaveth her virtue. That it is so, is apparent by the Eclypse of the Moone, for such as the substance such is the shadow: effected by the naturall preferring of all parts to the Center; if not of the World, yet of her owne body. For the former is denied by Copernicus and his followers, who would rather place the Sunne in the Center: & alleadging the Moone to be a heavy body, with rising and depressions, like our vallies and mountaines as since discovered by *Galileos* Glasses. And perhaps to a Menippus in the Moone, the Earth, according to Aristotle, would appeare another such Planet. Our poet before described the earth to hang in the Ayre, ballanced with her owne weight: and *Lucretius* of the same under name of Cybel:

> The sage Greek Poets sung, that she was by
> Yok't Lyons in her Chariot drawne on high
> By which they taught that this huge masse of mold
> Hung in the Ayre: nor earth could earth uphold.[28]

> Yet would the Ayre give it way, were it not at rest in her proper Center. Some have marveiled that it fell not: but that fall would have proved an ascension; for, which way soever, it must have fallen into heaven; which our Hemisphere would have done as soone as the other. Yet *Lactantius* and *S. Augustine* with acerbitie deride the opinion of the Antipodes, as if men could goe with their heads downward, and the raine upward; but heaven is every where above us, and upward and downeward are only words of relation in sphericall bodies, the superficies on every side, being the extreame, and the middle the Center. Yet *Virgilius* Bishop of *Salsburg*, was deprived of his Bishopricke for maintaining this opinion: now discovered by daily navigations, as long since by reason.[29]

In its lucid prose and its care to make everything clear to the Latinless reader, as in its fundamental conservatism and respect for authorities, this passage is representative of Sandys's commentary. It may also represent his age; I know few clearer examples to refute the popular notion that seventeenth-century man needed only to learn to use his eyes for the scales of medieval cosmology to fall away. The scientific revolution was a revolution of ideas, not observation.

But in the main Sandys is less interested in natural science than in politics and morality; "It should," we recall that he says, "be the principall end in publishing of Books, to informe the understanding, direct the will, and temper the affections." His political interpretations reveal a Machiavellian concern with the proper conduct of a prince and a desire to justify and analyze monarchy. Jove's parliament shows that "we may conclude with *Plato*, that the Monarchicall government is of all the best: the type of God, and defigured in the Fabrick of mans Body."[30] The fable of Phaethon "to the life presents a rash and ambitious Prince, inflamed with desire of glory and domination." The beasts of the zodiac who frightened Phaethon on his career across the sky are too powerful subjects, and the horses of the sun are the common people, "unruly, fierce, and prone to innovation: who finding the weaknesse of their Prince, fly out into all exorbitancies to a generall confusion."[31] The example of Actaeon shows "how dangerous a curiosity it is to search into the secrets of Princes, or by chance to discover their nakedness."[32] This last interpretation comes from Bacon's "Actaeon et Pentheus sive Curiosus" in the *De Sapientia Veterum*. Although Sandys toned down Bacon's Machiavellian realism in his interpretation of the myth of the River Styx, we cannot doubt that his careful study of Bacon's mythology explains why so many of his political interpretations have a realistic and monarchistic cast.[33] Experience of the Stuart court no doubt confirmed his study, or prompted it.

In his moralizing interpretations Sandys is more conventional, and his sources harder to trace in the windings and ramifications of Renaissance mythologies and Ovid commentaries. And why not? The old stories provided a wealth of illustrations and archetypes for truths which experience confirms. When Juno disguises herself as the nurse Beroe in order to deceive Semele, we learn that "No treachery is so speeding as that which makes under the visard of friendship."[34] Juno's peacock signifies "proud and ambitious men who attempt high things; riches, which morally is Juno, being their tutelar Goddesse; having need of many eyes to sentinell their wealth, and prevent their downfall."[35] Sandys took this interpretation from Natalis Comes's *Mythologiae*, that storehouse of eclectic interpretation.[36] But sometimes a myth generates its own interpretation so readily that no external source need be sought. Because the oracles of Themis were put in riddling language, the Thebans neglected them and preferred the easier oracles of the naiads. Who could mistake the meaning?

> The oracle of *Themis* signifies good and wholsom advice, (shee being the Goddesse of Counsel, perswading onely what is just and honest) as that of the *Naiades* foolish. So while the *Thebans* forsake the better to follow the worse, they draw on themselves a publique calamity: in all estates not rarely exemplified.[37]

No one can read Sandys's commentary without noticing how often and how enthusiastically he reconciles myth and scripture.

His own announcement of his efforts is altogether too modest. "[H]ere and there," he says in "To the Reader," he has given "a touch of the relation which those fabulous Traditions, have to the divine History, which the Fathers have observed, and made use of in convincing the Heathen." In fact, almost every page of his commentary shows an example of his eagerness to discover consonances between Ovid and holy writ. The myth of Astraea, who was taken up into heaven, perhaps alludes "to the righteous *Henocks* miraculous and early assumption."[38] The goddess Pallas Athena "is taken for the intelligence of *Jupiter*; (A notion, as some Authors report, derived by Tradition, of the second person, and soberly delivered by the *Sybils*, *Trismegistus*, and other Ethnicks, but after defaced by admixture of the Grecian vanities.)"[39] (Here again we notice Sandys's acceptance of Bacon's history of mythology, which held that the divine truths found in myths originated in a period of remote antiquity, after the Fall but before the "Grecian vanities" of classical times.) Stories like that of Apollo's love for Hyacinthus or Jupiter's for Ganymede, in which Marlowe took such evident delight, might have embarrassed Sandys's search for the germs of theology in Ovid. It was not to be so. "The Poets, shaddowing under their fables Philosophicall and Theologicall instructions, by the love of the Gods unto boyes expresse the graciousnesse of simplicity and innocency: and like little children, or not at all, must we ascend the celestiall habitations."[40] All in all, Sandys sees no reason to doubt that although Ovid may differ in some respects from Scripture, he yet "appeares in the rest so consonant to the truth, as doubtlesse he had either seene the Books of Moses, or receaved that doctrine by tradition."[41]

Bacon's attitude toward the reconciliation of the truths of myth and divinity differed radically from Sandys's. Bacon, we recall, believed that the truths found in myths were derived from the discoveries of ancient wise men in a time after the Fall and before any records known to modern man. The knowledge of these ancient sages had approached that of Adam before the Fall, and Bacon hoped that his *Instauratio* would restore man to this ancient and happy state of knowledge, which was the closest possible approximation to the irretrievable knowledge enjoyed by Adam when Word and World were one. Adam's knowledge had been physical, not theological:

> For it was not that pure and uncorrupted natural knowl-
> edge whereby Adam gave names to the creatures accord-
> ing to their propriety, which gave occasion to the fall. It
> was the ambitious and proud desire of moral knowledge
> to judge of good and evil, to the end that man may revolt
> from God and give laws to himself, which was the form
> and manner of the temptation.*

It followed then that the knowledge to be won from the myths
bore on the natural world and on man's ethical and political acts
rather than on the divine sphere.

In chapter 10 of the *De Sapientia Veterum*, "Actaeon et
Pentheus, sive Curiosus," Bacon finds in the myths themselves
an indication that those who investigate the nature of God as
though He were a problem in physics are doomed to failure.
Pentheus spied on the rites of Bacchus and was punished by the
god. This myth demonstrates that "the punishment assigned to
those who with rash audacity, forgetting their mortal condition,
aspire by the heights of nature and philosophy, as by climbing
a tree, to penetrate the divine mysteries, is perpetual inconstancy,
and a judgment vacillating and perplexed."[42]

Sandys could not accept Bacon's assertion that it was futile
to attempt to understand the divine mysteries. His handling of
the story of Pentheus shows how his thought diverges from
Bacon's on this point and at the same time how his careful study
of Bacon leaves traces throughout his commentary. Discussing
Pentheus's ascent of Cithaeron, Sandys digresses to provide in-
formation on the mountain: it is named after Orpheus's lyre or
cithara, because it was on Mt. Cithaeron that Orpheus initiated
the mysteries of Bacchus, which he had brought from Egypt. The
descendants of Ham had planted idolatry in this ancient land, and
from it the Greeks had taken many of their customs; Egypt, in
fact, with its traditions stretching back into an antiquity before
the flood, links the post-Adamic sages and classical antiquity. But
the traditions of Egypt are not to be preferred to the truth of

---

*   Neque enim pura illa et immaculata scientia naturalis, per quam Adam nomina
ex proprietate rebus imposuit, principium aut occasionem lapsui dedit. Sed
ambitiosa illa et imperativa scientiae moralis, de bono et malo diiudicantis,
cupiditas, ad hoc ut Homo a Deo deficeret et sibi ipsi leges daret, ea demum
ratio atque modus tentationis fuit (*Instauratio Magna* praef. = *Works* 1:32).

Genesis: "what Tradition delivers obscurely and lamely, is in the scripture entire and perspicuous."[43] Sandys follows this digression with a discussion of the politics of religious zeal as exemplified in the myth of Pentheus.

> There is nothing more plausible to the vulgar then the innovations of government and religion. To this they here throng in multitudes. Wise princes should rather indeavour to pacifie, then violently oppose a popular fury: which like a torrent beares all before it; but let alone exhausteth it selfe, and is easily suppressed. Reformation is therefore to be wrought by degress, and occasion attended: least through their too forward Zeale they reject the councill of the expert, and incounter too strong an opposition, to the ruine of themselves and their cause; whereof our Pentheus affords a miserable example. The blind rage of Superstition extinguisheth all naturall affection.

The main lines of this interpretation were suggested not by Bacon's interpretation of the Pentheus myth but by chapter 18 of the *De Sapientia Veterum*, "Diomedes, sive Zelus." There Bacon suggests that those who attempt to suppress a religious sect by violence rather than by reason, doctrine, and example "are by the vulgar (who can never like what is moderate) celebrated and almost worshipped as the only champions of truth and religion."[44] But their period of popular favor seldom endures, and if an alteration in the state brings the suppressed sect to power, the suppressors' honor turns to dust, and they are as hated as once they were glorified. Further, "the murder of Diomedes by the hands of his host alludes to the fact that difference in matter of religion breeds falsehood and treason even among the nearest and dearest friends."

In chapter 26, "Prometheus, sive Status Hominis," Bacon asserts not merely the futility of probing divine mysteries but the necessity of keeping separate the methods of human learning and divine. For making an attempt on the chastity of Minerva, Prometheus was sentenced to have his liver perpetually torn by vultures.[45] The Titan's crime and punishment illustrates the folly in learned men of trying to bring the divine wisdom itself under the dominion of sense and reason: from which attempt inevitably follows laceration of the mind and vexation without end and rest. And therefore men must soberly and modestly distinguish between things divine and human, between the oracles of sense and of faith; unless they mean to have at once a heretical religion and a fabulous philosophy.*

At the conclusion of his interpretation of the Prometheus myth, Bacon firmly rejects the harmonizing of myth and scripture which, as we have seen, plays so important a part in Sandys's commentary.

It is true that there are not a few things beneath which have a wonderful correspondency with the mysteries of the Christian faith. The voyage of Hercules especially, sailing in a pitcher to set Prometheus free, seems to present an image of God the Word hastening in the frail vessel of the flesh to redeem the human race. But I purposely refrain myself from all licence of speculation in this kind, lest peradventure I bring strange fire to the altar of the Lord.†

Sandys read Bacon's mythological writings, especially the *De Sapientia Veterum*, carefully and attentively. He accepted Bacon's view of the origin of myth in a post-Adamic, preclassical age of wisdom and used it to guide his own interpretation of Ovid. In the myths there is truth which it is the commentator's task to discover. This premise lies behind Sandys's decision to translate

---

* Illud non aliud esse videtur, quam quod homines artibus et scientia multa inflati, etiam sapientiam divinam sensibus et rationi subiicere saepius tentent; ex quo certissime sequitur mentis laceratio et stimulatio perpetua et irrequieta. Itaque mente sobria et submissa distinguenda sunt humana et divina; atque oracula sensus et fidei; nisi forte et religio haeretica et philosophia commentitia hominibus cordi sit (*Works* 6:675).

† . . . neque tamen inficiamur, illi subesse haud pauca, quae ad Christianae fidei mysteria miro consensu innuant; ante omnia navigatio illa Herculis in urceo ad liberandum Prometheum, imaginem Dei Verbi, in carne tanquam fragili vasulo ad redemptionem generis humani properantis, prae se ferre videtur. Verum nos omnem in hoc genere licentiam nobis ipsi interdicimus, ne forte igne extraneo ad altare Domini utamur (*Works* 6:676).

the *Metamorphoses* and influenced even the style of his verse. It is a premise received from Bacon, who may himself have been stimulated to form his theory by the preface to Comes's *Mythologiae*.

There was much, of course, in Bacon's mythology that Sandys ignored or rejected. His Baconian Machiavellianism, however moderated, and his emphasis on the moral and political truth in myths accompanies a lack of interest in systematic search for physical or scientific truths. Bacon would have seen this lack as an opportunity missed, especially since Sandys's wide travels and extensive acquaintance had allowed him to record a multitude of the observations on natural phenomena that were so essential to Bacon's scheme for the advancement of learning. Sandys thought of his work as essentially didactic and so emphasized one of Bacon's functions of myth, teaching difficult truths, at the expense of the other, concealing unpopular ones. Bacon would not have scorned this emphasis as emphatically as he would have deplored Sandys's constant reconciliation of myth and scripture. In Bacon's view, the two were better kept separated.

The differences between the two interpreters of myth go deeper still. Sandys chose to translate Ovid instead of some other ancient mythological author for, we may speculate, a variety of reasons: there is no more copious store of myths, the style commands admiration and provokes delight, the work had behind it a long tradition of interpretation, so that there was the attraction of seeing a familiar work in a new way. Sandys may have felt also that Ovid's varied and imaginative presentation of the myths would go well with his eclectic interpretation of them. Golding's version of 1565–1567 was no doubt beginning to show its age, and Sandys was fit to undertake its replacement. The translations that appear in *A Relation of a Journey* show him accomplished in translating various styles, and the travel book reveals his interest in antiquity. His admiration for Bacon may have had its roots elsewhere: in personal ties (his brother, Sir Myles Sandys, had been a member of Parliament for the University of Cambridge with Bacon in 1614)[46] or in a general acceptance of Bacon's rational approach to myth and belief that myths contained important truths.

But Sandys's choice of author might not have met with

Bacon's approval. References to Ovid are almost absent from Bacon's works, and his occasional oblique references to the kind of poetry represented by the *Metamorphoses* reveal a profound lack of sympathy for the unstable surface and fluid categories of the Ovidian universe. In Book 4 of the *De Augmentis Scientiarum*, for example, Bacon condemns the neo-Pythagorean doctrines that were the philosophical basis—insofar as one can talk of such a thing in this author—for Ovid's works. (As Sandys says, the teachings of Pythagoras set forth in *Metamorphoses* 15 contain a "diversity of changes agreeable to his [sc., Ovid's] argument") Bacon is discussing the doctrine that men have two souls, one corporeal and shared with brute beasts, the other spiritual, rational, and divine:

> Let there be therefore a more diligent inquiry concerning this doctrine; the rather because the imperfect understanding of this has bred opinions superstitious and corrupt and most injurious to the dignity of the human mind, touching metempsychosis, and the purifications of souls in periods of years, and indeed too near an affinity in all things between the human soul and the souls of brutes.*

Bacon's view of myth influenced Sandys's presentation of Ovid in outline and in detail. The very real differences between the two men's mythologies did not prevent Sandys from absorbing Bacon's ideas on the origin and purpose of myth, and those ideas resurface on almost every page of his commentary. Sandys was telling no more than the truth when he gave the Viscount St. Albans primacy in his list of authors. In comparison with Bacon's deep mark, the other authors in his list have only a broad, but superficial and intermittent, influence. To retrace Sandys's steps through his library from the track left in his commentary would teach one much about Renaissance learning and methods of reading, but the reward might turn out to be not worth the

---

* Itaque de hac doctrina diligentior fiat inquisitio; eo magis, quod haec res non bene intellecta opiniones superstitiosas et plane contaminatas, et dignitatem Animae Humanae pessime conculcantes, de Metempsychosi et Lustrationibus Animarum per periodos annorum, denique de nimis propinqua Animae Humanae erga animas brutorum per omnia cogitatione, peperit (*Works* 1:606).

effort. Sandys seems to have used the other authors as storehouses from which now one, now another interpretation could be drawn to add to his armory of understanding.

Consider his use of Regius and Sabinus, two of the best-known Renaissance commentators. In his interpretation of Achelous's story at the beginning of Book 9 we find on one page a story of Hannibal's meeting with Scipio that is found in Sabinus's notes on the passage, but not in Regius's.[47] On the next page the details and phrasing of Sandys's note on the strife between the Aetolians and Acarnanians reveal his dependence on Regius; the general rationalization of the myth is in Sabinus, but not the details.[48] "Eclectic," insofar as it implies a weighing of several possible interpretations and a final decision for one or another, is perhaps the wrong word for Sandys's procedure here. He stretches out his hand to Regius, then to Sabinus, then to another book and another. All interpretations are worthy of his consideration, and neither his Baconian belief in the ancient truth in myths nor his un-Baconian desire to reconcile myth and scripture obliges him to exclude anything he finds.

Sandys and the Revaluation of Ovid

By his willingness to include a variety of interpretations and information from a multitude of sources—ancients, moderns, church fathers, "a fellow, who six or seaven yeares had been a slave to the *Spanjard* in the *West-Indies*"[49]—Sandys places Ovid in the tradition of Renaissance polymathic poetry, of which Du Bartas's *Divine Weekes and Workes* is perhaps the best-known example. The title page of Thomas Lodge's *Learned Summary* (London, 1621) on that poem reveals the range of knowledge such poems were expected to embrace:

A Learned
SUMMARY
Upon the famous
*POEME of William of
Saluste Lord of Bartas.
Wherein are discovered all the
excellent secrets in Metaphysicall*

Physicall, Morall, and Historicall
knowledge.
Fitt for the learned to refresh theire me-
mories, and for younger students to abreviat
and further theire studies:
Wherein nature is discovered, art disclosed
and history layd open.

Lodge's claims (p. 2r) that in Du Bartas's compendium of knowl-
edge "the learned shall meete with matter to refresh their mem-
ories, the younger Students, a Directory to fashion their discourse;
the weakest capacity, matter of wit, worth, and admiration,"
would have been endorsed by Sandys as a description of his Ovid.

But Sandys and Lodge would have parted company over the
question of Ovid's value as an author "wherein are discovered
all the excellent secrets in Metaphysicall, Physicall, Morall, and
Historicall knowledge." Sandys, as we have seen, saw nothing
in Ovid's poetry incompatible with divine truth. Lodge, on the
other hand, rejected any suggestion that pagan writers might
convey the same truth that had been handed down in scripture.
"We are now falne into such a time," he wrote,

> wherein the study of Piety, of Sacred and true Antiquitie,
> of Liberall Sciences and true Philosophy, are misprized,
> & rejected. In their place Satans impostures are admitted,
> who by his subtilties hath in such sort bewitched the
> worst part of men, that nothing is in more esteeme with
> them, then that which is fabulous, and obscene; neither
> any thing in lesse repute then the fruitful lustre of truth.[50]

By "true Antiquitie" and "true Philosophy" Lodge means the
biblical subject and theological doctrine of his admired Du Bartas,
"as much delightful as any Greeke, Latine, or French Author that
we can light upon." He might have prayed as did Josuah Sylvester
in his translation of Du Bartas:

> O! furnish me with an unvulgar style.
> That I by this may wain our wanton Ile
> From Ovid's heires, and their un-hallowed spell
> Here charming senses, chaining soules in Hell.

Sylvester's translation, which Douglas Bush has called "the epic of middle-class Protestantism,"[51] and Lodge's *Learned Summary* represent one aspect of a rejection of Ovid and Ovidian poetry which took place in the early seventeenth century. Sandys's 1632 *Metamorphosis* defiantly reasserted Ovid's claim to be taken seriously. His Baconian Ovid was to be for the seventeenth century what the allegorical Ovid had been for the fourteenth: a source of truth, endorsed by its consonance with that revealed in scripture.

Sandys on one side and Lodge, Sylvester, and their master Du Bartas on the other resume an old debate which was taking on fresh energy in the early seventeenth century. Whether Christians should have anything to do with pagan arts and letters, animated as these were by a mythology to which Christianity professed itself both alien and superior, was a question which had exercised Tertullian, and the debate had continued, waxing or waning in intensity, to Sandys's day.[52] Ovid's *Metamorphoses* came into the debate early on and was impelled to the center by its position as the most copious and readable source of pagan myths. But here the general question of the compatibility of Christian doctrine and pagan culture assumed a particular form. As with the similar case of Virgil's Fourth *Eclogue* and its resemblance to the messianic prophesies of Isaiah, the striking agreement between the narrative of *Genesis* and Ovid's account in *Metamorphoses 1* of Creation and the Deluge led thoughtful men to wonder whether the whole *Metamorphoses* could be shown to be consonant with scripture. The anonymous *Ovide moralisé* and the *Metamorphosis Ovidiana moraliter...explanata* ascribed to "Thomas Walleys," the latter widely read in the early sixteenth century, exemplify the results of this speculation.

But during the sixteenth century the belief that the *Metamorphoses* were the Bible through a glass, darkly, began to seem old-fashioned, even faintly ridiculous. The twenty-eighth letter in the collection of *Epistulae Obscurorum Virorum*, which was published in 1515 or 1516, satirized the practice of reading the *Metamorphoses* as a multi-level allegory. Petrus Lavinius, whose tropological analysis of the *Metamorphoses* routinely graced Renaissance editions, cut short his accommodation of Ovid to scripture with the first book, as did Golding in the verse letter accompanying his translation. The parallel between *Metamorphoses* 1 and *Genesis* was too obvious to reject. The sixteenth century's tendency to go no further in discovering parallels was a harbinger of the seventeenth century's eventual rejection of the allegorical tradition which had given life and color to early Renaissance art. Allegory finds and often forces correspondences between superficially dissimilar things. Its structure, rigid but frail, could not stand up to the seventeenth century's growing demand for truth absolute and directly apprehended. Both scientific rationalism and Puritan hostility toward paganism sprang from this desire to know what is actively and directly, without interference from authority or superstition.[53]

Against the seventeenth century's rejection of Ovid, or rather of the allegorical interpretation of Ovid, Sandys set his 1632 *Metamorphosis*. Far from being a late flowering of the allegorical interpretation, his Ovid showed how ancient myths could be compatible with the new desire to know divine truth as directly as possible. Bacon's interpretation of myth was the key to Sandys's new Ovid. By showing that pagan mythology preserved truths revealed to man in a time before the Flood and passed down in a twin stream, lucidly through divine scripture and opaquely in heathen myth, Bacon demonstrated that an author like Ovid could be used as a vehicle to carry men to the truth. Bacon's and Sandys's interpretation of myth is not quite the same as the old allegorical reading. The allegorical reading asserted that by Deucalion, for example, is signified Noah; Sandys and Bacon saw in Deucalion a representation of the same divine truth that is delivered in the story of Noah. Scripture, of course, is true and plain; myth is false, heathenish, and requires interpretation. But behind both lies divine truth, and it was on the path leading to that truth through Ovid that Sandys wished to set his readers.

We should not overestimate the originality of Sandys. Just as he took his theory of myth from Bacon, so he had a predecessor in his assertion that a pagan author, translated and interpreted, could lead men to divine truth. George Chapman in the epilogue to his *Iliads* of 1611 lifts Homer as near to scripture as any pagan book could be:

But where our most diligent Spondanus ends his worke

with a prayer to be taken out of these Meanders and Euripian rivers (as he termes them) of Ethnicke and prophane writers (being quite contrarie to himselfe at the beginning), I thrice humbly beseech the most deare and divine mercie (ever most incomparably preferring the great light of his truth in his direct and infallible Scripture) I may ever be enabled, by resting wondring in his right comfortable shadows in these, to magnifie the clearnesse of his almighty appearance in the other.

Chapman, like Sandys, believed that the author he was translating could be read as a vehicle for divine truth, a "comfortable shadow" of scripture's bright light. In both translators the idea can be traced to Ficino and the *prisca theologia* of the Florentine Neoplatonists. Chapman, a pricklier character and a better poet than Sandys, sets himself more emphatically against his predecessors in interpretation. His rejection of Spondanus in the passage just quoted is of a piece with his scorn for earlier translators and commentators in his letter "To the Reader" prefixed to his *Iliads*. Sandys no less than Chapman was concerned to offer a new valuation of his author, but he announced his intention by declaring his adherence to Bacon, not by rejecting earlier commentators.

There is another way in which Chapman may have showed Sandys how a translation could work against the prevailing view of the translated author. Sandys believed that his author's style was important because it was the medium through which the truth-bearing myths came down to us. His author presented truth which is God and from God, inspired by divine poesy: "Phoebus Apollo (sacred Poesy) / Thus taught: for in these ancient Fables lie / The mysteries of all Philosophie." Chapman had similar views on Homer's style. It was as divine as Homer's matter: "Then let lie / Your Lutes and Viols, and more loftily / Make the Heroiques of your Homer sung; / To Drums and Trumpets set his Angel's tongue."[54] Truth in Chapman's view is inseparable from poetry and equally perfect:

> And, as in a spring
> The plyant water, mov'd with any thing
> Let fall into it, puts her motion out
> In perfect circles, that move round about

The gentle fountaine, one another raising:
So Truth and Poesie worke, so Poesie, blazing
All subjects falne in her exhaustlesse fount,
Works most exactly, makes a true account
Of all things to her high discharges given,
Till all be circular and round as heaven.[55]

Chapman, it has long been recognized, was one of the first to reject the poetic use of mythology as mere decoration,[56] and in his emphatic linking of "Truth and Poesie" he revealed that he shared the desire of many in the early seventeenth century to know the truth as directly as possible. But Chapman, and Sandys as well, differed from writers like Lodge and Sylvester in that, far from being reluctant to break with paganism, they willingly embraced pagan poetry as a vehicle of truth.

In asserting, then, that a pagan author could be a vehicle for divine truth, Sandys was doing nothing that Chapman had not done before him. But by putting forward Ovid as such a vehicle Sandys sets himself in opposition to two developments in English poetry of the late sixteenth and early seventeenth centuries. The popularity of the Ovidian eroto-mythological poem during the last quarter of the sixteenth century assured that the seventeenth century's rejection of pagan frivolity would be a rejection of Ovid as well. The rejection of Ovid against which Sandys set his 1632 *Metamorphosis* can often be seen in the career of a single writer. The same Thomas Lodge who inveighed against pagan writers in his commentary on Du Bartas's *Divine Weekes and Workes* wrote as a young man *Scillae's Metamorphosis: Enterlaced with the unfortunate love of Glaucus* (1589). Together with Marlowe's *Hero and Leander* and Shakespeare's *Venus and Adonis*, it established the Ovidian erotic and mythological poem as an important mode of expression. These elaborately wrought narratives may carry a certain amount of conceptual baggage, but they are designed to flash through the reader's mind, leaving a trail of color behind. Delight rather than instruction is their purpose.[57]

And delight, as we have seen, was viewed with increasing suspicion by the time Sandys set out to translate the *Metamorphoses*. The Ovidian eroto-mythological poem had died or been transformed. Sandys may have wondered if it was not possible to transform Ovid's great poem of transformation itself and to turn it from a source of delightful pagan tales into a source of divine truth. Here too Chapman, as he had in making his translation of Homer into a kind of scripture, may have pointed the way to Sandys. His transformation of the Ovidian eroto-mythological narrative from a celebration of sensual pleasures into a vehicle for the exposition of divine truth, seen in the contrast between *Venus and Adonis* and *Ovid's Banquet of Sense* or between Marlowe's *Hero and Leander* and Chapman's continuation, showed what a translation of the *Metamorphoses* might become.

Another aspect of the anti-Ovidian trend in poetry of the early seventeenth century may be seen in the rise of "metaphysical" poetry. Despite the difficulties of formulating an exact definition for this adjective, it is still possible to chart in early seventeenth-century lyric a movement away from mythological referents and toward direct experience, away from allegory and toward conceit, away from narrative style and toward dramatic.[58] If Ovidian matter appears in these poems, it is subordinated to genuine feeling, human conflict, and movement toward point and paradox, as in John Cleveland's "The Antiplatonick":

> What though she be a Dame of stone
> The Widow of *Pigmalion*;
> As hard and un-relenting she,
> As the new-crusted *Niobe*;
> Or what doth more of statue carry,
> A Nunne of the Platonick Quarry!
> Love melts the rigour which the rocks have bred,
> A flint will break upon a Feather-bed.

Like the Puritan epic poets and the scientists, the Metaphysicals sought to know the truth directly and from experience. They had little use for decorative mythology, allegory, or the Ovidian manner.

By 1620, then, the English-speaking world was ready for a new *Metamorphoses* to replace Golding's late medieval version of more than half a century before. The allegorical tradition was dead; so too was the erotic and mythological poem on Ovidian themes. The search for truth that could be directly apprehended was beginning to shape not only religion and science but also poetry and the interpretation of ancient myth. In this situation nothing less was needed than a revaluation of Ovid's *Metamorphoses*. It is often true, especially in the case of classical authors, that when we approve or disapprove of an author we are responding more to critical tradition about the author and to this reputation than to any inherent qualities. It is also true that a translation, representing as it does a fossilized critical reading and a total transformation of a work from an alien to a familiar dress, may prompt readers to look at a work anew. Sandys's *Metamorphosis* offered such a revaluation.

But simple translation, the presentation of English verses that would describe the same events and mimic the rhetorical colors of Ovid's Latin, would not, however well done, give the world a new *Metamorphoses*. Indeed, a simple translation might mislead the world into believing that Sandys wanted to be numbered among those heirs of Ovid whom Sylvester had criticized. Sandys was not reworking Ovid but rather the Ovid tradition. For him the myth, not the medium, was the message; like Bacon, and unlike Chapman, he was more interested in the ancient stories and the truths behind them than in the author by whom they had been handed down to us. Hence his decision to add to the bare translation of 1626 the elaborate apparatus of prose explanations, marginal glosses, and engraved plates of the 1632 edition. All these must be taken as part of the "text." Sandys himself declares in his dedication "To the King" that this apparatus gives intellectual life to his translation: "To this have I added, as the Mind to the Body, the History and Philosophicall sense of the Fables (with the shadow of either in picture). . . ."

Sandys's parenthesis deserves some consideration, for it suggests yet another way in which Sandys's text offers the reader a revaluation of the Ovid tradition. Editions of Ovid had been decorated with simple woodcuts before, but the engravings in Sandys's *Metamorphosis* were unprecedented in their elaborate compression of a book's events onto a single page and in their integral place in his text. Through them, he implies in his introduction, the reader—for these plates must be read, not seen— might attain an understanding of the myths beyond that given by the word:

> And for thy farther delight I have contracted the sub-
> stance of every Booke into as many Figures... since there
> is betweene Poetry and Picture so great a congruitie; the
> one called by Simonides a speaking Picture, and the other
> a silent Poesie: Both Daughters of the Imagination, both
> busied in the imitation of Nature, or transcending it for
> the better with equall liberty: the one being borne in the
> beginning of the World; and the other soone after, as
> appeares by the Hieroglyphicall Figures on the Aegyptian
> Obelisques, which were long before the invention of
> Letters: the one feasting the Eare, and the other the Eye,
> the noblest of the sences, by which the Understanding
> is onely informed, and the mind sincerely delighted....

The Neoplatonic tenet of vision's primacy among the senses, the
citation of Simonides' epigram, and above all the reference to
hieroglyphs suggest an affinity between Sandys's plates and the
Renaissance emblem-book.[59] Certainly Sandys's remarks to his
readers imply a power for his plates beyond anything claimed
by Sir John Harington, despite the strong resemblance in style
and layout between Sandys's figures and the illustrations to
Orlando Furioso:

> The use of the picture is evident, which is that (having
> read over the booke) you may read it (as it were againe)
> in the very picture, and one thing is to be noted which
> everyone (haply) will not observe, namely the perspective
> in every figure. For the personages of men, the shapes
> of horses, and such like, are made large at the bottome
> and lesser upward, as if you were to behold all the same
> in a plaine, that which is nearest seemes greatest and the
> fardest shewes smallest, which is the chiefe art in
> picture.[60]

From a dozen or so feet away, even a sharp-eyed person might
be pardoned for mistaking one of Harington's plates for one of
Sandys's. Both would show mythological or heroic figures
grouped in actions from the book, the earlier episodes in the
foreground and the later spiraling away into the distance. But
the two translators expected their readers to make very different

uses of their figures. Looking at Harington's illustrations would simply recapitulate the action of the book, whereas Sandys's emblematic figures would *sincerely* delight the mind through their appeal to the eye, "noblest of the sences, by which the Understanding is onely informed." The "farther delight" which Sandys promises his readers is no purely sensual pleasure.

Many reasons might be given to account for the difference between Harington and Sandys: the development, charted by Rosemary Freeman, of the emblem tradition in England, or even the fact that as illustrated books became widely available in the early seventeenth century, readers became more sophisticated in their ways of looking at illustrations. (Even so, Harington's delighted explanation of the trick of perspective must have seemed naive in 1591.) But Sandys's belief in the emblematic power of his illustrations owes less to these general causes than to his personal belief in the truth of ancient myths. Because the old stories contain the truth, they are valuable of themselves and give the value of truth to whatever rightly conveys them—Ovid, Natalis Comes, or Sandys's engravings. The engravings have a power like that of the "Hieroglyphicall Figures on the Aegyptian Obelisques," and the fables themselves, as Sandys tells us earlier in the same passage, resemble those same hieroglyphs:

> I have attempted . . . to collect out of sundrie Authors the Philosophicall sense of these fables of Ovid; if I may call them his, when most of them are more antient then any extant Author, or perhaps then Letters themselves; before which, as they expressed their Conceptions in Hieroglyphickes, so did they their Philosophie and Divinitie under Fables and Parables.[61]

Ut pictura poesis, in fact, but in Sandys's hands the trope has Bacon's stamp on it. "As hieroglyphics were before letters, so parables were before arguments"; further, pictures and translated verses are alike because they share in the truth of the ancient stories which they convey. The medium, the style or manner in which they are conveyed, is important only insofar as it reveals or obscures the truth in the myth.

It is easy to exaggerate the degree to which Sandys's *Metamorphosis* represents a reworking of the view of Ovid's *Metamorpho-*

ses current when he began the translation. Much in his commentary is conventional, Neoplatonic, Boethian, Hermetic, Christian and humanistic, and might be found in works written forty years before, or, though less frequently, forty years after 1632. Sandys no less than Bacon shows the paradoxical Renaissance cast of mind wherein commonplace and unoriginal doctrines become the vehicles of dearly won, deeply held, original belief. Sandys's Ovid would not have been unintelligible to Golding, but it would have given the older translator much to think about.

Yet Sandys's belief that in the myths Ovid is telling the truth, and that the truth, not Ovid, is what matters, sets him apart from previous interpreters of the *Metamorphoses* and from Chapman, his predecessor in revaluing Ovid. This belief, as I have tried to show, arose out of Sandys's careful reading of Bacon's mythological works, especially the *De Sapientia Veterum*. Sandys makes and sustains a far more sweeping claim for the value of his author than any previous English Ovidian. In transforming Ovid from a medieval *auctour* whose works might be read as allegories of moral and scriptural truth or as sources of encapsulated wisdom (*Ovidius sententiarum floribus repletus*, as Hugh of Trimberg called him) into a modern author whose myths were as near as mortals after Adam could come to the wisdom of the ancients, Sandys helped Ovid to pass unscathed through the change of taste that in prose cast the copious and moral Cicero out of fashion and replaced him with the terse, pointed Seneca. Readers in the seventeenth century cared more and more for truth told directly and less and less for adornment. Sandys showed them how Ovid might seem true, or suggest truth. John Aubrey records that "reading of Ovid's *Metamorphy* in English by Sandys" was a wonderful help to his imagination, and that his friend Francis Potter conceived the idea of transfusing the blood while reading Ovid's story of Jason and Medea.[62] In his palaeontological writings Robert Hooke placed Ovid's views of the origin of the world beside the evidence of fossils, for he valued him as heir to "the most ancient and most knowing Philosophers among the Aegyptians and Greeks."[63]

4

Sandys's Style
The Sentence Inforceth

All truth is from God, but the manner and means of our knowing it are variously understood. Sandys, following Bacon, believed that ancient myths preserved the mysteries of philosophy, truth inherited from an antediluvian age when man's knowledge of the world approached as nearly as possible Adam's ideal and simultaneous knowledge of Word and World. Just as man after the Fall could not recover Adam's knowledge, so after the Deluge man no longer understood the truths of the ancient sages of the previous era. In the myths of the Greeks, however, and in the even more ancient, as was believed, hieroglyphs of the Egyptians, these truths were imbedded. Rightly interpreted, the myths would yield up their treasure.

Sandys also, following Chapman's identification of Homer's truth with Homer's poetry, believed that poetry, which is divine, acted as an intermediary or conductor of truth between its divine origin and human understanding. The myth of Apollo's presidency of the Muses reflects this relation between poetry and divine truth: "*Jupiter* the divine mind, inspires *Apollo*; *Apollo* the Muses; and they their legitimate issue."[1] Truth can be found in Ovid because it is in the fables which Ovid narrates, and Ovid's poetry presents those fables in a form closer to their divine origin than would prose, for

> . . . verse hath a greater efficacy then prose: which penetrates deeper, and makes a more lasting impression. For as the voice passing through the narrow conduit of a trumpet breakes forth more cleare and musicall: even so

the sence contracted by the strict necessity of numbers. The other is heard with more negligence, and lesse impulsion: but when the excellent matter is restrained in measures, the same sentence not only allures but inforceth.[2]

This statement on poetry, which is consistent with Sandys's other pronouncements on the subject, reveals an approach to the process of putting words together radically different from our ideas on translation. The translator may imitate in his style the effect of his original, he may write a poem such as his author would have written were he alive in the translator's day, he may simply express the meaning of his author in natural and fluent style. Sandys in fact did all these things and was praised for them. Dryden, to whom we owe many of our unconscious assumptions about literary translation, commended Sandys for giving to his verse the same turn it had in the original, a talent not found in every poet. An anonymous panegyricist suggests that future critics will suppose, "When Naso afterwards arrives their hands, / Ovid hath well translated English SANDS."[3] Drayton lauded Sandys's fluent smoothness in "To My Most Dearely-Loved Friend Henery Reynolds Esquire, of Poets and Poesie":

Then dainty *Sands* that hath to *English* done
Smooth sliding *Ovid*, and made him run
With so much sweetnesse and unusual grace,
As though the neatnesse of the English pace,
Should tell the Jetting Lattine that it came
But slowly after, as though stiffe and lame.

Because Sandys wrote in an Ovidian, natural, fluent manner, critics from his own day on have praised him for these qualities without considering why he chose such a style.

The failure of Sandys's first critics to appreciate the intellectual underpinning of his style may perhaps be attributed to the fact that Sandys, caught here too between two worlds, wrote in the future and thought in the past. The heroic couplet which he used and helped to develop became the standard medium for almost every kind of poetry in the next century and a half.[4] At the same time Sandys's thought on the nature and function of verse was rooted in ideas about the nature of poetry and the world which were old-fashioned in 1632 and which fifty years after must have seemed echoes from a remote past. Who in the 1680s would have seen more than a pretty conceit in Sandys's picture of Apollo at the center of the Muses, "playing so harmoniously on the instrument of this world, moving in order and measure, and consorting with every part; so that by his meanes there is no dissonancy in nature"?[5]

Sandys identified Apollo with poesy in the "Minde of the Frontispiece, and Argument of this Worke." If this picture of the god is no mere conceit but a true statement of the relation between poetry and the cosmos, then style becomes a matter of real importance. Poesy as it plays the instrument of the cosmos draws forth and gives expression to the harmony that inheres in the instrument; at the same time, it can be said to create that harmony because its central position in the cosmic order ensures the absence of dissonance. Human poetry can share in the power of this cosmic harmony; by creating a music which is in microcosm the macrocosmic music of the universe, verse can purge our souls of dissonance. The thought of this power of verse is enough to make any poet think twice before putting one word after another.

The translator also must remember the real power of harmonious words when he sets about his task. Although he works at several removes from the origin of truth, his imitation of his author's expression of the Muses' inspiration which comes from Apollo who has it from the mind of God, still partakes of some of the power of its origin. "When the excellent matter is restrained in measures, the same sentence not only allures but inforceth." The power of poetry to enforce changes in the reader's mind is akin to the power of earthly music to produce alterations in the listener's state of mind. Both verse and music participate in the cosmic power of Music, the Muses' province.

Hence the necessity for care in choice of style. First, of course, the power of poetry might mislead:

> But who ever heard a Swan sing? A fiction invented by *Greece*, the mother of fables, perhaps to beautify their Poems. For such is the sweetnesse and power of Poesie,

as it makes that appeare, which were in prose both false and ridiculous, to resemble the truth; and with such an incredible delight imprints it in the mindes of the hearers, as cannot be easily out-raced.[6]

Poetry can make the false seem true; conversely, therefore, it could also make the true seem false. Bad verse—that is, verse that poorly imitates the cosmic harmony—might fail to enforce its meaning on the reader's mind. Thus the translator has a special burden. If truth is to be found in the author being translated, then the translator must not stand between his readers and that truth. His style must invoke not only his author's power but also the power of Music to conduct the truth to his reader's mind and to call forth harmonies there that will impress the truth. But how?

"Sweetnesse and power" are not concepts that we would ordinarily link except in oxymoron, but Sandys's concept of poetry makes their association natural. Powerful verse must be sweet, that is, smooth and harmonious, because its power comes from its harmony which the poet has designed in imitation of the cosmic harmony. We are so accustomed when talking about language and its effects to use words like "impression," "penetrate," and "efficacy" in an extended or metaphorical sense that we can easily overlook the fact that Sandys is not speaking metaphorically when he says that "verse hath a greater efficacy then prose: which penetrates deeper, and makes a more lasting impression." Verse free of discord and harmonious in its numbers can by imitating the cosmic harmony draw upon its power and work changes in those who hear. The structured sound of verse, like the streams of minute particles that Hobbes postulated as the immediate cause of sense impressions, was to work a real, physical change in its audience.

Sandys stands in the not unfamiliar position of a man who bases his actions on one set of principles only to have them attributed to another set entirely. "It should be the principall end," he wrote, "in publishing of Bookes, to informe the understanding, direct the will, and temper the affections." Hard words, it may be, for post-Romantic readers to understand; there is nothing about style, nothing about the need to say something to the reader or about the reader's response, nothing about beauty, art, or nature. Sandys's statement seems authoritarian, leaving little room for the reader's freedom of response.

To an eighteenth-century reader the statement would have been less disturbing; after all, literature existed to express universal truths, and these truths were expected to have a moral application. But still the reader was expected to assent to the truths voluntarily. The writer's virtues, lucidity and smoothness, were meant to make the reader's understanding easier, not to force a change in the physical structure of the reader's mind. Sandys wrote, in fact, at the moment when style was beginning to be seen as a separate literary entity, something personal to an author and separable from the content of his work. In his effort to make the music of his verse conform to the divine Music of the universe, he helped smooth and polish the medium, the closed couplet, that was to dominate verse for the next century and a half. Because his verse looks forward in this way, it has too often been assumed that his theory of poetry must also reflect the growing awareness of style.

And just as Sandys in his commentary cites the latest scientific discoveries and news from the New World, so he at times seems to suggest that style can be considered apart from content. In this paragraph from "To the Reader," smoothness of style seems to be merely another aid to the reader, in the same class as marginal notes:

> To the Translation I have given what perfection my Pen could bestow; by polishing, altering, or restoring, the harsh, improper, or mistaken, with a nicer exactnesse then perhaps is required in so long a labour. I have also added Marginall notes for illustration and ease of the meere English Reader, since divers places in our Author are otherwise impossible to be understood but by those who are well versed in the ancient Poets and Historians; withall to avoid the confusion of names which are given to one Person, derived from his Ancestors, Country, Quality, or Achievements. The heads of the stories set in capitall letters in the Margent of the Translation are the same with those in the margent of the Commentary: by which you may readily find the Mythologie peculiar unto every Fable.

Similar though this statement is to the claims of smooth-running verse made by the poets of a century later, its context and background are far different.

The paragraph falls between Sandys's explanation of his recovery of truths from Ovid which are also found in scripture and his explanation of the Simonidean efficacy of his plates. The entire essay presents Sandys's Ovid to the reader in a conceptual package constructed of Neoplatonic, Aristotelian, and Horatian elements. Plato is cited on the importance of fables in leading the young to virtue; Sandys agrees with Aristotle that "the Poet not onely renders things as they are; but what are not, as if they were, or rather as they should bee"; he maintains that painter and poet resemble one another, "the end of the one and the other being to mingle Delight and Profit." This mix in two pages would not have seemed strange to one of Marlowe's fellows. Dryden's contemporaries might have thought it curiously old-fashioned in prose criticism. Imitation and the parallel between poetry and painting continued to be topics in criticism even long after Dryden, but their force was transformed by neoclassicism.

Sandys rarely comments at all on the style of the author he is translating, and when he does he expresses himself in the vaguest terms. His comment on the oratorical contest between Ajax and Ulysses for Achilles' armor, though unusually full, is rhetorical rather than literary criticism. Sandys admires Ovid for his ethopoeia, and his comment would not seem out of place in the mouth of Quintilian:

> In this contention for the armor, that difference is arbitrated, how the courage of the mind, and strength of the body, is of lesse use in affaires of warre, then councell and policy; the one personated in *Ajax*, and the other in *Ulysses*. Wherein our Poet hath admirably suted the words to the matter, and both to the quality of the persons. *Ajax* oration is souldier-like; vehement, disdainefull, boasting of his birth and glory of his actions: *Ulisses*, on the other side, composed, rhetoricall, and prevalent to his purpose; by which he obtaineth the armor.[7]

More typical in brevity and vagueness are the following judgments in Ovid's style. There cannot be many others in all Sandys's commentary. Mercury and Jupiter were entertained by Philemon and Baucis, "whose homely and hearty entertainment is most conceitedly expressed by our wittiest of authors." Nearing the end, Sandys allows himself a sigh of relief: "Now are wee in sight of shore: arrived at the last book of this admirable Poem. Wherein his Muse flags not (the infelicity almost of all other Poets) but rather flies a more lofty pitch, both in matter and expression." Our first judgment remains unmodified: Sandys did not concern himself with style as an entity separate from content, something which could be smoothed and polished for the sake of some beauty inherent in it alone. His striving after correctness does not arise from some vague belief that correct verse is prettier verse. Smoothness and polish were important to Sandys only insofar as they worked a change in the reader's mind and compelled him to accept the truths that were in the myths. Sandys believed that he was translating myths, not Ovid. He wished to show the lightning, not the lightning rod.

Poets, however, should never be allowed the last word on their work, and we may legitimately ask, as Sandys would not have asked, what features distinguish the style of his *Metamorphosis*. About the importance of one aspect of his style there can be little doubt—and little added here. Without question Sandys's *Metamorphosis* played a seminal role in the development of English "Augustan" poetic diction and shaped the rhetoric and meter of the heroic couplet.[8] A selection of couplets will show how balanced and correct Sandys can be:

Tritonia to the Muse attention lends:
Who both her Verse, and just revenge commends.

Nor dwelling, nor her nation fame impart
Unto the Damsell, but excelling Art.
Derived from *Colophonian Idmons* side;
Who thirstie Wooll in *Phocian* purple dide.

The boy then twelve years aged; of a minde
Apt for instruction, and to Arts inclind.[9]

It is worth pointing out that lines like these owe their inspiration to an obvious feature of Ovid's style, his fondness for balance and wordplay within a line. Imitation of Ovidian balance, moreover,

does not always produce an Augustan line. When Sandys writes
a couplet like this:

> And now uncar'd for odours powr'd upon her;
> And undue death with all due rites doth honour,

he seems Mannerist rather than Augustan, closer to the Donne
who wrote,

> Death I recant, and say, unsaid by me
> Whate'er hath slipped, that might diminish thee,

than to Dryden or Pope. But he is only imitating Ovid's rhetorical
flourish, *ut tamen ingratos in pectora fudit odores / et dedit
amplexus iniustaque iusta peregit.*[10]

Likewise, comparison of Sandys's English with Ovid's Latin
does not yield up any such harvest of delights as that farrago of
blunders and felicities which is Marlowe's *Amores*. Places where
Sandys can be said to have improved Ovid are rare, and it is hard
to discover any place where he has failed to understand the Latin
as the scholarship of his time presented it to him. Of improve-
ments, one example: at *Metamorphoses* 9, 131ff. Ovid records the
dying words of the centaur Nessus and his gift to Heracles' wife
Deianira of the tunic soaked in venomous blood which would
later kill Heracles:

> excipit hunc Nessus: "neque enim moriemur inulti"
> secum ait, et calido velamina tincta cruore
> dat munus raptae velut inritamen amoris.

Sandys's version shifts Nessus's last statement from indirect to
direct discourse and changes the centaur's first thought into a
sinister whisper:

> This *Nessus* tooke; and softly said: yet I
> *Alcides*, will not unrevenged dy.
> And gave his Rape a robe, dipt in that gore:
> This will (said he) the heat of love restore.

Ovid's rather colorless *secum ait* and *velut inritamen amoris* have
become transformed in Sandys's more vivid version.

In talking about Sandys's style we must ask whether we are
discussing one thing or several. Students of Sandys have carefully

considered whether there is any difference between the style of the 1621, 1626, and 1632 editions, and whether there is any progressive change in style between the earlier and later books of the 1632 edition. To both questions the answer is yes, but not significantly.[11] Only for the first five books, of course, can we compare three versions. When we do, it is clear that the changes, though numerous, are minor. In Book 5 I have counted twenty-one changes from the 1621 to the 1626 version and fifteen changes from the 1626 to the 1632 version. Most of these are trivial refinements of spelling (e.g., "suffize" to "suffice" or "eger" to "eager"); the rest are improvements based on a new understanding of the Latin text or of Ovid's mythological allusions. To follow them is to see Sandys at work.

Ovid, planting metamorphosis within metamorphosis, inserts into the story of Ceres' search for Proserpina the tale of a slave (*puer*) who mocked the goddess and was changed into a lizard for his insolence. In his new shape he fled from the old woman at whose cottage Ceres had stopped. The old lady, understandably confused, marvels and weeps and tries to catch him, all at once: *Mirantem flentemque et tangere monstra parantem / fugit anum latebramque petit.* So Sandys translated in 1621: "a Lizard, th' aged wife / (That wonders, weeps, and strives to take it) shuns, / And presently into a crevise runs." By 1626, however, he had consulted a text which read, as Sabinus, Regius, and most Renaissance editions do, *paventem* for *parantem* in line 459. Convinced, he altered his translation to read "wonders, weeps, and feares to touch it."[12] Modern editors prefer *parantem*, which is supported by the most authoritative manuscripts, to *paventem*, but Sandys, at a time when textual criticism was a considerable art but an infant science, cannot be blamed for following the most learned editors of his day.

When he revised his translation, Sandys was careful to check not only text but also commentary. In the 1621 and 1626 editions he translates *Metamorphoses* 5, 327–28 as follows: "*Jove* turned himselfe, she said, into a Bull: / Whence *Libyan Hammon* hath a horned scull." Ovid, lest he seem to condescend to readers who knew full well what animal's horns Jupiter Ammon bore, does not specify: "*Duxque gregis*" dixit "*fit Iuppiter; unde recurvis / nunc quoque formatus Libys est cum cornibus Ammon.*" In revising the translation for the 1632 edition, Sandys consulted Regius's commentary and discovered his mistake. Regius explains *duxque gregis* thus: *periphrasis est arietis. Nam iuppiter se in arietem commutavit.* Sandys made the necessary change, although the new rhyme was not even as exact as the old: "*Jove* turn'd himselfe, shee said, into a Ram: / From whence the horns of *Libyan Hammon* came."[13]

These examples, along with changes made purely for the sake of smoothness, like the revision of "Which in the middle doth his nares divide" (1621 and 1626) into "Which doth his nostrils in the midst divide" (1632, p. 174), illustrate what Sandys meant when he said that he had revised the translation "by polishing, altering, or restoring, the harsh, improper, or mistaken, with a nicer exactnesse then perhaps is required in so long a labour." Anyone who has ever gone through a lengthy classical text comparing the various readings of the manuscript tradition, tracking down allusions, and identifying proper names will sympathize with the note of weariness in Sandys's words. When we consider in addition the task of revising an already successful translation, our respect for Sandys as a scholarly translator must grow. We also see how important the *Metamorphoses* were to him. Ovid's work was no mere collection of pretty tales. God was in the details; divine truth conveyed by divine poesy made the *Metamorphoses* worth this painstaking labor in addition to the great task of equipping each book with its commentary.

Taken together, however, the changes do not amount to enough that we should regard the text of the 1632 edition as different in any significant way from its predecessors. Within the 1632 text itself careful readers have noticed slight changes in Sandys's style from first to last. A count made nearly a century ago showed a progressive increase in enjambment from the first book to the last. Fourteen percent of the lines in Book 1 are unstopped, and 29 percent in Book 15. Of couplets, only 1.8 percent of those in the first book are unstopped, compared to 10.4 percent in the last.[14] Although Books 11 and 12 happen to have a higher percentage of unstopped couplets than Books 13, 14, and 15, the fact of Sandys's increasing willingness to use enjambment remains secure. My count, made before I consulted Wood's study, showed a steady numerical increase in unstopped couplets: one in Book 3, four in 6, five in 9, eleven in 12, and fourteen in 15. More than that, the increase is noticeable, something that strikes the reader even without the prompting of numerical analysis.

The same is true of Sandys's use of alliteration, which becomes increasingly obvious and frequent as we move from Book 1 to Book 15. Sometimes, especially in the earlier books, Sandys used alliteration in strict imitation of Ovid's use. Describing Europa in Book 6, lines 105–7, Ovid writes:

> Ipsa videbatur terras spectare relictas,
> Et comites clamare suas, tactumque vereri
> Assilientis aquae, timidasque reducere plantas.

Sandys translates:

> Back to the shore she casts a heavy eye;
> To her distracted damsels seemes to cry:
> And from the sprinkling waves, that skip to meet
> With such a burden, shrinks her trembling feet.[15]

Here "distracted damsels" (there is no warrant for the epithet in the Latin) is simply an attempt to reproduce the effect of Ovid's *comtes clamare*. But by Book 11, to give only one instance, Sandys has become willing to use alliteration far in excess of anything in the Latin:

> And even as fowle whose feet intangled are
> Within the subtile fowlers secret snare
> Become by fearful fluttering faster bound.[16]

Nothing like the profusion of fluttering fricatives graces Ovid's simile:

> Utque suum laqueis, quos callidus abdidit auceps,
> Crus ubi commisit volucris sensitque teneri,
> Plangitur, ac trepidans astringit vincula motu.

Despite these slight changes from the early books to the later, the 1632 edition is best treated as a whole and may, as Davis says, "safely be used as representative of Sandys's fundamental characteristics in metre and rhetoric over the whole period of his composition."[17]

Rhetoric and Compression

What are these characteristics? Some—Sandys's liking for balance and antithesis within a line, his selective vocabulary, his handling of caesura—have been amply discussed by the scholars who have established Sandys's place in the development of the heroic couplet. Here I hope to point out some other features of Sandys's style and show how they might have arisen as solutions to the problem of translating Ovid. Two characteristics, or rather two characteristic concerns of the translator Sandys, immediately confront our inquiry: Sandys's care in translating the obvious features of Ovid's rhetoric, and his attention to what we may call the problem of compression.

Sandys's education at school and university taught him to see Ovid as a rhetorician's quarry of tropes and figures. And in England the doctrine was gaining strength that held that poetry was not incidentally but essentially like rhetoric, that, as George Puttenham said, poetry was "a manner of utterance more eloquent and rethoricall then the ordinarie prose which we use in our daily talke, because it is decked and set out with all maner of fresh colours and figures."[18] It is not surprising, therefore, that these rhetorical devices find their way into his translation; after all, they were part of Ovid for him.

In Book 2, Ovid tells the story of how Mercury stole Apollo's cattle. An old countryman, one Battus, happened to see the theft, and Mercury swore him to silence. Later, to test the old man's good faith Mercury returns in disguise and bribes him to betray the location of the cattle.

> "rustice, vidisti signas hoc limite," dixit
> "ire boves, fer opem furtoque silentia deme!
> iuncta suo pariter dabitur tibi femina tauro."
> at senior, postquam est merces geminata, "sub illis
> montibus" inquit "erant, et erant sub montibus illis."
> risit Atlantiades et "me mihi, perfide, prodis?
> me mihi prodis?" ait periuraque pectora vertit
> in durum silicem, qui nunc quoque dicitur index,
> inque nihil merito vetus est infamia saxo.[19]

Sandys has carefully preserved not only the repetitions in Ovid's

Latin but even the position of *sub illis*, which he translates by a redundant "there."

> Detect the theft; in their recoverie joyne:
> And lo, this Heifer, with her Bull, is thine,
> He (the reward redoubl'd) answer'd: There
> Beneath those hills, beneath those hills they were.
> The, Hermes, laughing lowd: What, Knave, I say,
> Me to my selfe; me to my selfe betray?
> Then, to a touchstone turn's his perjur'd brest;
> Whose nature now is in that name exprest.

Sandys adds a marginal note on the rhetorical device: "Such vaine and superfluous repetitions were called in Greeke *Battalogie*: from whence *Battus* an idle Poet, is here covertly attacked by *Ovid*."[20] Under the name "turn," the repetition was commended by English critics from Puttenham on. The turn is concisely defined by Anthony Blackwall in his *Introduction to the Classics* of 1718:

> The most charming *Repetitions* are those, whereby the principal Words in a Sentence, either the same in Sound, or Signification, are repeated with such Advantage and Improvement, as raises a new Thought, or gives a musical Cadence and Harmony to the Period. Those in *English* are call'd fine *Turns*; and are either upon the words only, or the Thought, or both.[21]

As Dryden observed, "Virgil and Ovid are the two principal fountains of them [sc., turns] in Latin poetry."[22] Later he withdrew Virgil's name.[23]

Sandys evidently judged the figure to be of some importance, for in that complex calculus in which translators must engage he had decided to carry over the length of the passage (eight lines) and the dominant rhetorical device at the expense of Ovid's concluding *sententia*. Lines 706–7 in the Latin depend on our recognizing that *index* can have two meanings: "touchstone" and "tattler." A literal translation of the two-and-one-half lines might be "He turned his perjured heart into hard flint, which is now called *index*, and on the underserving stone is still the ancient slander." Sandys compresses the two-and-a-half lines into two and passes over Ovid's personification of the slandered stone. Indeed,

Ovid's play on the double meaning of *index* would be lost entirely
if Sandys did not explain in the margin how it happens that the
touchstone's "nature now is in that name exprest." "The touch-
stone," he says, "is called *Index*: which also signifies an
Intelligencer, or tel-tale."

Sometimes Sandys's attention to Ovid's rhetoric leads him to
preserve in his translation the high rhetorical coloring of lines
that modern critics, and ancient ones too, might wish muted.[24]
The odd, jingling rhymes and repetitions in

> The gold-haired mother of life-strengthning Seed,
> The snake-hair'd mother of the winged Steed
> Found thee a stallion[25]

reflect Ovid's sledgehammer alliteration at the lines' end and his
balance of *te . . . mater sensit equum . . . te sensit equum . . . mater*:

> Et te flava comas frugum mitissima mater
> Sensit equum: te sensit equum crinita colubris
> Mater equi volucris.

(Again I quote the Renaissance vulgate; modern editions have
sensit volucrem for *te sensit equum*.)

At other times the imitation of Ovid's rhetoric helps Sandys
to achieve a corresponding excellence of his own. Niobe's speech
over the corpses of her seven sons killed by Latona's son Apollo
is a small masterpiece of Ovidian character-drawing through
rhetoric.[26] Niobe's grief, as first heard in the moaning long *u* and
o sounds of *crudelis, nostro, Latona, dolore*, is mixed with and
gives way to anger at the jealous goddess, expressed by the
anaphora of *pascere . . . pascere* and the change from moaning
vowels to the taunting assonance of *exsulta . . . inimica triumpha*.
Repetition with epanorthosis (*victrix . . . cur autem victrix?*)
conveys Niobe's hubristic reversion to her old scorn of Latona,
and the balanced opposition of *miserae mihi . . . tibi felici* and the
paradox of *post tot . . . funera vinco* underline her determination
to set herself against the goddess. Then, in plain words slowly
stretched against this speech, once more the bowstring sounds:

> "pascere, crudelis, nostro, Latona, dolore,
> pascere" ait "satiaque meo tua pectora luctu!

corque ferum satia!" dixit. "per funera septem
efferor: exsulta victrixque inimica triumpha!
cur autem victrix? miserae mihi plura supersunt,
quam tibi felici; post tot quoque funera vinco!"
Dixerat, et sonuit contento nervus ab arcu.[27]

Sandys, despite the weak "subdew" forced as a rhyme of "few,"
matches Ovid's miniature excellence:

Cruell Latona, feast thee with our harmes:
Feast, feast, she said, the salvage stomack cloy;
Cloy they wild rage, and in our sorrow joy:
Seaven times, upon seven Herses borne, I dy.
Triumph, triumph, victorious foe. But why
Victorious? haplesse I have not so few:
Who, after all these funeralls, subdew.
This said, the bow-string twangs....[28]

He has recognized the rhetorical art in Ovid's speech and trans-
lated it with rhetorical art of his own. Ovid's modulation of vowel
sounds, difficult to reproduce in English, is gone, and the one tone
of Niobe's speech in Sandys's version is uniform: anger. Taking
his cue from Ovid's repetition of *pascere* and *victrix*, Sandys binds
the speech together with a complex pattern of repetition and
anastrophe (feast...Feast, feast; cloy / Cloy; Seaven...seaven;
Triumph, triumph, victorious...Victorious). Ovid's concluding
device, the paradox of *post tot funera vinco*, becomes the animat-
ing device of Sandys's version. "In our sorrow joy" has no coun-
terpart in Ovid's Latin, and the suggestion of a pun in "borne,
I dy" strengthens the fundamental note of paradox. Niobe is still
victorious, ahead of Latona in number of children, even after her
seven sons have been killed.

The pun in "borne, I dy" when compared with the Latin
paronomasia it translates, illustrates the strength and weakness
of Sandys's effort to translate Ovid's rhetoric by matching figure
for figure. *Efferor* can mean "I am carried (in funeral procession)"
or "I am carried (in triumph)." Ovid's Niobe says *per funera
septem efferor*, "I am myself carried out for burial in these seven
funerals." But the imperative *triumpha* at the end of the line
makes us realize that the sentence has another meaning: "In these

deaths I triumph seven times." Even so, not until we have finished
Niobe's speech and reflected on the transformation from moaning
grief to hubristic anger which it revealed do we recognize *efferor*
for what it is: the first note of the modulation, unheard by Niobe
but a sign to us of the persistence of her desire to set herself over
Latona. This dynamic use of rhetorical figures to reveal character
does not find its way into Sandys's translation. He renders thought
with thought, paronomasia with paronomasia, *per septem funera
efferor* with "upon seaven Herses borne, I dy." The last three
words, paradoxical in isolation, add nothing by their paradox to
any development of Niobe's character.

Perhaps our regret at Sandys's failure to render Ovid's pre-
sentation of character as it changes, and the failure itself, are
inevitable. Translations, after all, are fossilized readings, and
every age reads in different ways. Sandys, taught from his school
days to read Ovid for his wealth of rhetorical figures, naturally
thought those figures important enough to translate. Our own
age, hostile to rhetoric, is taught from the elementary stages of
literary study to value ambiguity and the flow and movement
of a poem. With Ovid, the impulse to play on the meanings of
efferor may have come from a different, private source: his
fascination with changing states, metamorphosis, and his need
to fix in words the moment of transition from one state to
another. Further, our perception that Sandys has failed to do
something interesting that Ovid did should not blind us to the
excellence of Sandys's translation here. It is not all that Ovid is,
but it is Ovidian—smooth, balanced, and rhetorical. And in com-
pensation for Ovid's dynamic fusion of rhetoric and character-
ization, we have Sandys's static but complete presentation of
Niobe's grieving anger and the almost lyric strength he gives to
her utterance by his repetition of key words and by his variation
of caesura and use of intital trochees in lines like "Cloy thy wild
rage, and in our sorrow joy." Most important of all, Sandys has
kept the main effect: Niobe's exultation, and then the sound of
the bow again.

Any translator from Latin to English faces what I have come
to think of as the problem of compression. Latin is an inflected
language with a polysyllabic vocabulary, while English has a
syntax dependent on word order and a vocabulary full of essential

monosyllables, "the dead weight of our mother tongue," as Dryden called them.[29] Hence one word in Latin tends to become several in English: *portabatur*, beginning students learn, means "it was being carried." Further, a translator turning Latin dactylic hexameters into English heroic couplets faces a continual need to compress, for the six feet of the Latin line may have as many as seventeen syllables, as in Virgil's *pulverulenta putrem sonitu quatit ungula campum*, whereas the five feet of the English iambic line cannot vary by more than one or two syllables from ten. An ingenious translator can do much to fit his English to the scale of Latin, but almost inevitably the English translation is longer than its Latin original. Sandys turns Ovid's 12,000 lines into more than 13,100. Even so, almost every page of his translation bears the marks of his effort to keep his version in proportion with its original. Scale is part of truth, and a bloated Ovid would be no representation of truth.

One device, often overlooked, by which Sandys attacks the problem of compression is his apparatus of commentary, both the full-scale commentaries at the end of each book and the briefer marginal comments. This apparatus should be taken as part of Sandys's text. As we read the 1632 *Metamorphosis*, in fact, the commentaries demand a rather different mode of reading from their predecessors, the Renaissance Ovid commentaries of Regius, Sabinus, or Micyllus. In Renaissance large-format editions, with which Sandys's small folio of 1632 is most fairly to be compared, Ovid's verse is surrounded by commentary in prose. The text floats in a sea of linguistic, historical, literary, and philosophical information. The notes may be by one scholar or several; if by several, the commentators' contributions are distinguished by their names in the margin. The effect of this format, I suggest, is to focus the reader's attention on Ovid and to subordinate the commentary to Ovid's words. Lighting on a page of such an edition, the eye beholds a few lines of Ovid resting in splendid isolation, their importance stressed by larger type, within a dense border of undifferentiated, unlemmatized commentary set in smaller type. One's impulse is to read the Ovid and consult the commentary selectively, in case of difficulty.

We know hardly anything about the physical act of reading in times past—so little, in fact, that assertion in this area is necessarily subjective. We are likely to remain forever ignorant of how people's eyes moved over a page in the sixteenth and seventeenth centuries, how long it took them to read ten lines of Ovid in Regius's edition. It may be significant, however, that a great many of the notes in Renaissance Ovid commentaries are clearly intended to help the reader with discrete points of difficulty that may have arisen in reading the poetry. Obscure words are glossed, mythological allusions explained, and rhetorical figures analyzed. It is natural to suppose that if the reader was not troubled by the difficulty, the note went unconsulted. There is some evidence, also, to indicate that Renaissance readers did not read every word of the commentary before them. Marlowe used Dominicus Niger's commentary in making his translation of the *Amores*, but he used some notes and ignored others, even when a glance at them might have helped him.[30] In translating *Amores* 1.5 he adroitly fuses text and gloss in the first line. In his text he found *Aestus erat, mediamque dies exegerat horam.* Niger comments on *aestus*, "hot": *Aestus, ut & aestatis tempus, quo propter noctes breviores solent homines meridiari, ostenderet.* Niger's suggestion that *aestus* implies *aestas* becomes part of Marlowe's translation: "In summers heate, and midtime of the day." Marlowe did not, however, read in Niger's commentary as far as the top of the second column on the next page, for he would have found there a note on *venit* in line 9: *Praesentis est temporis.* He renders *venit* by a past tense, "Then came Corinna."

Sandys's apparatus serves a different purpose and calls forth from the reader a different response from those Renaissance editions of Ovid which it superficially resembles. For one thing, the text to which Sandys's apparatus is attached is a translation, and his own. The fact that commentary and text commented on owe their existence to a single maker, Sandys, gives to the commentary a status almost equal to that of the text. The reader is less likely to ignore any part of the apparatus when he is aware that both spring from a single intention. Apparatus and translation both represent Sandys on Ovid, and both are intended to help the reader toward the ancient truth which Sandys saw as the most important reason for reading, translating, or commenting upon Ovid. Sandys's introduction shows that he gave much attention to the design and layout of the 1632 edition. His very disposition of translation and apparatus also gives to his commentary a status, a claim on the reader's attention, almost as strong as that of the translation. As we read through the book we do not have the option of taking in the words of Ovid on any single page and ignoring the modern commentary. The commentary stands between each book of the translation and demands our undivided attention. Marginal keywords join each fable in the translation to the corresponding section of the commentary, but the narrative form of Sandys's comments and his lucid, readable prose discourage page-flipping. By a paradox of book design, the physical separation of text and commentary encourages the reader to see them as closely connected, two parts of a single work.

Treating his commentary in this way allows Sandys to use it as part of his solution to the problem of compression. His apparatus acquires an ambiguous status which he can exploit to expand the limits imposed by the need to keep his translation in due proportion with its original. If every translation is in a sense a commentary on its original, revealing what the translator sees as essential and important, it is equally true that there is a sense in which a commentary may become part of a translation. Certainly these lines—not Sandys's best—would be unintelligible, or at least difficult, to someone who did not have the explanation which Sandys provides:

> When in this fabrick *Minos* had inclosed
> This double forme, of man and beast composed;
> The Monster, with Athenian blood twice fed,
> His owne, the third Lot, in the ninth yeare, shed.

Marginal notes identify the "third Lot" as Theseus and direct the reader to the commentary for an explanation of the Minotaur's double form. Used in this way, the apparatus becomes part of the translation and yet not part of it. I have already pointed out how in translating *Metamorphoses* 2.707 Sandys relies on the marginal notes to convey to his readers the point of an Ovidian *sententia* for which there was no room in his translation proper. Others could be added. Sandys can imitate Ovid's concise allusiveness, confident that his apparatus will save him from falling into obscurity. Reading Sandys's comments, we are not reading his translation of Ovid, yet we cannot read his translation of Ovid without reading his comments.

Sandys's effort to keep his translation in just proportion with its original left its mark most firmly in his verse. It has long been recognized that his contribution to the development of the heroic couplet springs in part from his attempt to reflect in English the smoothness, balance, and conciseness which he found in Ovid. As Ruth Wallerstein says, "Sandys in his whole verse and not merely in sententious passages, with a deliberate technique translated the rhetoric of Ovid into forms suited to the idiom of English speech and built upon the structure of the closed and epigrammatic couplet."[31] Wallerstein is concerned with the relation between Sandys's rhetorical expression and his metrical units and with the development of a system of closed couplets with prevailingly closed lines and a medial caesura. "In the development of this style," she says, "he is highly original, for although he found in Ovid many suggestions for this rhetoric and design, what is in Ovid a general method of thought, Sandys has stylized into a pattern of rhetorical and musical expression." Ovid is not, in my judgment, any less stylized than Sandys, and it is perhaps better to speak of Sandys as translating one patterned mode of expression into another. What seems in Sandys to be stylization is in fact the effect produced by the contrast between on the one hand Ovid's highly developed rhetoric, rich in figures of expression, and his flexible verse structure, and on the other hand Sandys's more restrained rhetoric and less variable meter— the contrast, leaving aside all consideration of the personal contributions of Ovid or Sandys, between the full palette and three colors. Here I shall point out two of Sandys's resources which have been passed over by previous critics: his use of amputated sentences, and his composition in verse paragraphs. Both are devices for compression, and both are inspired, though in rather different ways, by Ovid.

By "amputated sentences" I mean one- or two-word utterances, often grammatically incomplete or with the most tenuous connection to the surrounding sentences, used at the beginning of a line. They are characteristic of Sandys's style but do not seem to have been much used by later writers of heroic couplets. Cephalus' account of his hunting expedition in Book 7 displays the device:

> Arm'd with this dart, I solitary went,
> Without horse, huntsmen, toyles, or dogs of sent.
> Much kild; I to the cooler shades repair:
> And where the vallie breathes a fresher aire.[32]

It is tempting to see such an amputated sentence as an attempt to turn into English the brevity and syntactic independence of the Latin ablative absolute. In fact, ablative absolutes do not occur in the Latin originals of the present passage or of most of the others where Sandys uses amputated sentences. "Much kill'd" compresses an elaborate Ovidian periphrasis: *sed cum satiata ferinae / dextera caedis erat* ("but when my hand had had its fill of the slaughter of wild creatures," says the Loeb translator). The use of amputated sentences may have been suggested to Sandys by such elliptical formulae of transition as *tum secum* (6.3) or *nec mora* (e.g., 4.481) or by such formulae as *dixerat* (4.291) or *inquit* (4.476 *et passim*), but there is no sign that Sandys is seeking to imitate specific phrases when he employs amputated sentences.

Rather, he is trying to compress Ovid's meaning into an English that will have very nearly the same number of lines as the Latin. For the first eight lines of Book 6 he is able to stay with Ovid line for line, but in order to do so he must introduce an acephalous sentence in line 5:

> *Tritonia* to the Muse attention lends
> *Praebuerat dictis Tritonia talibus aures*
> Who both her Verse, and just revenge commends.
> *Carminaque Aonidum iustamque probaverat iram;*
> Then said t'her selfe: To praise is of no worth:
> *tum secum: "laudare parum est, laudemur et ipsae*
> Let our revengefull Powre our praise set forth.
> *numina nec sperni sine poena nostra sinamus."*
> Intends *Arachne's* ruin. She, she heard
> *Maeoniaeque animum fatis intendit Arachnes,*
> Before her curious webs, her own preferr'd.
> *quam sibi lanificae non cedere laudibus artis*
> Nor dwelling, nor her nation fame impart
> *audierat. non illa loco nec origine gentis*

> Unto the Damsell, but excelling Art.
>   *clara, sed arte fuit.*

In this case Sandys pays too high a price for compact and Ovidian proportions. "Intends *Arachne's* ruin" appears cramped and poor next to Ovid's spacious, balanced *Maeoniaeque animum fatis intendit Arachnes*, and even if we forgive the loss of an ornamental epithet and a pleasant framing of the line by noun and adjective, the English does not mean quite the same as the Latin, for *animum intendit* means "directs her attention to," not "resolves on" or "intends." The momentary uncertainty over the antecedents of "she" and "her" also distracts the reader's attention and weakens the line.

At times, however, Sandys does use amputated sentences to imitate a concise expression in Ovid. King Aeacus's description of pestilence in Aegina from Book 7 contains two examples within eight lines:

> The Bore forgets his rage: swift feete now faile
> The Hart: nor Beares the horned Heard assaile.
> All languish. Woods, fields, paths (no longer beare)
> Are fild with carkasses, that stench the aire.
> Which neither dogs, nor greedy fowle (how much
> To be admir'd!) nor hoary wolves would touch.
> Falling consume: which deadly Odors bred,
> That round about their dire contagion spred.[33]

"All languish" translates *omnia languor habet*, and "Falling consume" renders, though with a slight change in the relation of tenses and an unusual intransitive use of "consume," *dilapsa liquescunt*. In Sandys's day "consume" could be intransitive, as at the Authorized Version, Job 13.28, "Hee, as a rotten thing consumeth, as a garment that is motheaten." But the transitive use is far more common at all periods.

Amputated sentences were not a successful device for solving the problem of compression and so are rightly excluded from lists of Sandys's contributions to the heroic couplet. They remain a striking but idiosyncratic feature of his style. A less striking feature, and one which emerges only when his English is compared with Ovid's Latin, is his practice of translating by verse-paragraphs. It would have been easy to assume that the best way to produce a translation in scale with the original would be to make sure that each line of the translation corresponds to a line of the original. But line-for-line translations are seldom successful, and Sandys did not make the mistake of attempting one. To confirm his rejection of this way of translating he had ancient authority and the weight of poetry's analogy with painting; as he said in the dedication to his translation of Grotius's *Christus Patiens*,

> There is a Fault, which Painters call, *Too much to the Life*.
> *Quintilian* censures One, that he more affected Similitude
> than Beauty; who would have shewn greater Skill, if less
> of Resemblance. The same in Poetry is condemned by
> *Horace*, of that Art the great Law-giver.[34]

Marlowe's example would have been enough to deter him from line-for-line translation, even if he had understood the purpose of Marlowe's rearrangement of Ovid. But there is no sign that Sandys read Marlowe; his translation of the famous couplet *vilia miretur vulgus* etc. from *Amores* 1.15 shows no signs of Marlowe's influence.[35] Instead, Sandys chose to translate Ovid in such a way that the number of lines in each short section of his verse would match, as far as possible, the number of lines in the corresponding section of Ovid's. If a line were lost along the way, it might be gained back by the end of the paragraph.

A clear instance of this kind of translating can be seen in Sandys's treatment of part of the description of the palace of the sun in Book 2 of the *Metamorphoses*.[36] For the first four lines Sandys matches Ovid line for line:

> Sol's loftie Palace on high Pillars raised
>   *Regia Solis erat sublimibus alta columnis*
> Shone all with gold, and stones that flamelike blaz'd.
>   *clara micante auro, flammasque imitante pyropo*
> The roofe of Ivory, divinely deckt:
>   *cuius ebur nitidum fastigia summa tegebat,*
> The two-leav'd silver doores bright raies project.
>   *argenti bifores radiabant limine valvae.*

Then one line in Ovid has to become two in Sandys:

> The workmanship more admiration crav'd:

> For, curious *Mulciber* had there ingrav'd
>> *materiam superabat opus, nam Mulciber illic*

But in compensation the next two-and-one-half lines of Ovid become two in Sandys:

> The Land-imbracing Sea, the orbed ground
>> *Aequora caelarat medias cingentia terras,*
>> *terrarumque orbem,*
> The arched heavens. Blew gods the billows crown'd
>>> *coelumque quod imminet orbi:*
>> *caeruleos habet unda deos,*

and by changing the order in which the sea-gods are listed by Ovid, Sandys is able to fit the final two-and-one-half lines of Latin into two of English, thus concluding the passage in the same number of lines, ten, as Ovid used;

> Shape-changing *Proteus*, *Triton* shrill; the tall
>>> *Tritona canorum*
>> *Proteaque ambiguum,*
> Big-brawn'd *Aegaeon* mounted on a Whale.
>>> *balaenarumque prementem*
>> *Aegona suis immania terga lacertis.*

By making the paragraph or group of lines rather than the single line his unit of translation, Sandys was able to keep his translation close to the scale set by Ovid and at the same time avoid the awkwardness inevitable in a line-for-line translation. Sandys thus widened the field of a translator's vision and showed that elegance could be gained with no loss in accuracy if a translator would keep in mind the entire passage being translated, and not just one or two lines.

The final lines of the passage just analyzed illustrate Sandys's willingness to depart, though not excessively, from the order of presentation set by his original. He seems to have been criticized for this license, for in his marginal comment on the names of Actaeon's dogs—one of the few passages, incidentally, where Golding's influence can be seen—he says, "The transposition of these names in divers places to sute with the numbers, have caused some to taxe there interpretations."[37] But there can be no doubt that Sandys's way of translating became usual, and that translations like Golding's, which had been reprinted as recently as 1612, were rendered obsolete at once by the appearance of Sandys's version. An extreme example may best point up the contrast between new and old modes of translation. Contrast these lines from *The Fable of Ovid treting of Narcissus* with Sandys's version:

> This man the fearfull hartes, inforcying to his nettes,
> The caulyng nymphe one daye, behelde that nether ever lettes
> To talke to those that spake, nor yet hathe power of speche
> Before by Ecco this I mene, the dobbeler of skreeche.

I have already shown that the anonymous translator is slavishly following the order of ideas in Ovid's Latin:

> aspicit hunc trepidos agitantem in retia cervos
> vocalis nympha quae nec reticere loquenti
> nec prior ipsa loqui didicit, resonabilis Echo.

Sandys gives up the Latin order and writes:

> The vocall Nymph, this lovely boy did spy
> (She could no proffer speech, nor not reply)
> When busie in persuit of salvage spoyles,
> He drave the Deere into his corded toyles.[38]

This is not Sandys's best manner ("vocall" is a perfunctory choice for *vocalis*, and "lovely," which corresponds to nothing in the Latin, is a feeble epithet) nor his worst; it is, however, clear and smooth and has a certain grace.

In turning his attention from the single phrase or line to the paragraph or passage, Sandys was perhaps following the lead of Ovid and attempting to imitate the style of the *Metamorphoses* as he had imitated its rhetorical devices. Certainly the hexameters of the *Metamorphoses* give a very different effect from the elegiac couplets of Ovid's other works; as John Barsby sums it up, "The verse itself flows smoothly and easily, freed from the jerkiness of the end-stopped elegiac couplet; the reader is carried along by the preponderance of dactyls, the rarity of harsh elisions, the regularity of the caesuras, the co-ordinate sentence structure, and the frequency of enjambment (whole passages can sometimes be read without significant punctuation)."[39] When Sandys sought to perfect his translation by "polishing, altering, or restoring, the harsh, improper, or mistaken," he perhaps—one cannot be sure— had in mind these evident qualities of Ovid's style in the *Metamorphoses*. His increasing use of enjambment and alliteration as the work progressed may also have grown from a desire to spur his verse to an Ovidian pace.

Without doubt Sandys could translate at a different pace when he felt it right. His version of Hugo Grotius's steady trimeters in the *Christus Patiens* has a heavier, more formal accent than his Ovidian versions in the same meter. Despite the rhyme, there is something Miltonic in the pace as well as the subject matter of these lines:

> Those damned spirits of infernal Night,
> Rebels to God, and to the Sons of Light
> Inveterate Foes; my voice but heard, forsake
> The long possest; and, struck with Terrour, quake.
> Nor was't enough for Chirst, such wonders done,
> To profit those alone who see the Sun:
> To vanquish Death, my powerful Hand invades
> His silent Regions, and inferiour shades.[40]

There is something, too, reminiscent of Chapman in the highly enjambed decasyllabic couplets and long, complex sentences.

If we turn our attention back to a passage quoted earlier (p. 94), we can see a third of Sandys's devices for solving the problem of compression: the epithet. In that passage Sandys rendered Ovid's *aequora caelarat medias cingentia terras, / terrarumque orbem, coelumque quod imminet orbi* as "... ingrav'd / The Land-imbracing Sea, the orbed ground, / The arched heavens." Under pressure of the need to make up ground lost against Ovid earlier in the passage, Sandys has concentrated a participial phrase, *medias cingentia terras*, into a compound epithet, "Land-imbracing," and he has reduced a relative clause, *quod imminet orbi*, to the simple "arched." From a means of reducing Latin to the necessary dimensions of English, the epithet became a multipurpose tool of Sandys's style. Not only compression but antithesis, balance, alliteration—all these and more could be achieved by judicious invention and disposition of epithets. Since the use of epithets has long been recognized as one of Sandys's important contributions to the diction of the English heroic couplet, there is no need for detailed discussion here.[41] An extended quotation will display the variety in choice and placement of Sandys's epithets. It will further serve as a good, and concluding, example of his most vigorous, rapid manner. The passage from Book 3 of the *Metamorphoses* describes the death throes of the dragon killed by Cadmus:

> The hardenesse of his skin, and scales that growe
> Upon his *armed* back, repulse the blowe.
> And yet that *strong* defense could not so well
> The vigour of his *thrilling* Dart repel;
> Which through his *winding* back a passage rends:
> There sticks: the steele into his guts descends.
> *Rabid* with anguish, he retorts his looke
> Upon the wound; and then the javelin tooke
> Betweene his teeth; it every way doth winde:
> At length, tugg'd out, yet leaves the head behind.
> His rage increast with his *augmenting* paines:
> And his *thick-painting* throte swels with *full* veines.
> A *cold white* froth surrounds his *poys'nous* jawes:
> On *thundring* Earth his *trayling* scales he drawes:
> Who from his *black* and *Stygian* maw eject's
> A *blasting* breath, which all the ayre infect's.
> His body, now he circularly bends;
> Forthwith into a *monstrous* length extends:
> Then rusheth on, like *showr-incensed* Floods;
> And with his brest ore-bears the *obvious* Woods.[42]

Literalness and compression, Douglas Bush suggested some years ago, were the goals whose pursuit helped Sandys to purge and refine the heroic couplet and give it the final shaping before it passed into the hands of Dryden and Pope.[43] I have shown that Sandys's literalness can be understood as an attempt to imitate the figures and colors of Ovid's rhetoric, which Sandys's education would have taught him to identify as an essential part of reading Ovid. Further, I have pointed out several of the devices that Sandys uses to effect compression in his translation and

shown how these devices come to characterize his style. It re-
mains to suggest what Sandys's literalness and compression have
to do with the central assumption in his interpretation of Ovid:
the Baconian belief that in the myths reported by Ovid lay truths
discovered by wise men of preclassical antiquity.

It must be emphasized that any suggestion of direct relation-
ship between Sandys's Baconian mythology and his style in the
couplets of his Ovid translation can only be speculation. Sandys
does not say much about his style, and what he does say tends
to be laconic and conventional. Nevertheless, I think we can see
a relationship between the mythology and the verse style. It may
be objected that there need be no relation at all, that the com-
mentaries on each book were written after the translation and
published only in the third edition, and that the style of the
translation may be merely Sandys's way of writing couplets. To
refute the latter objection it is enough to point to the very
different couplets of Sandys's translation of the *Christus Patiens*.
As for the former, even though the commentaries were written
after the translation, the reading on which they are based must
have occupied more than the busy years between Sandys's com-
pletion of the translation, probably sometime in 1625, and the
appearance of the 1632 *Metamorphosis*. In particular, the influ-
ence of Bacon on Sandys's idea of myth is deep and systematic,
not limited to borrowings in specific cases. Sandys must have
studied Bacon's writings intensively and deeply.

The connection, then, between the literalness and compres-
sion which mark Sandys's style and his Baconian view of myth
is simply this: in the myths told by Ovid, Sandys believed, were
to be found truths about man and the world of which he was
the measure. These truths had been conveyed to the first makers
of myth by the divine spirit of poetry, the same who is repre-
sented in the myths as Phoebus Apollo: "Phoebus Apollo (sacred
Poesy) / Thus taught: for in these ancient Fables lie / The mys-
teries of all Philosophie." It follows, therefore—and in this Sandys
departs from Bacon—that the poetry itself, the manner of telling
the myth, was an essential part of the myth's truth. Hence as
much as possible of that poetry must be kept in translation.
Literalness preserves the rhetoric of Ovid, and for Sandys, as for
almost every practitioner and theorist of verse between George

Puttenham and Samuel Johnson, rhetoric was an essential characteristic, perhaps *the* essential characteristic, of poetry. Compression too was necessary. It preserved the scale of Ovid's work and prevented the insertion of expansions and translator's statements like those that stamped Chapman's Homer or Sylvester's Du Bartas with the mark of their translators. Sandys had no desire to intrude his personality between the reader and Ovid:

> To this [sc., providing the apparatus of commentary and plates] I was the rather induced, that so excellent a Poem might with the like Solemnity be entertained by us, as it hath beene among other Nations: rendred in so many languages, illustrated by Comments, and imbelished with Figures: withall, that I may not prove lesse gratefull to my Autor, by whose Muse I may modestly hope to be rescued from Oblivion.

For what he had to say about Ovid, the commentary provided ample scope.

Sandys, translating a divinely inspired text, faced the same problem as the translators of the Authorized Version of the Bible. They believed that their original had been animated more directly than Sandys's by the divine breath and were accordingly all the more aware of the need to suppress any expression of the translator's personality in the work. For translating the word of God "there were many chosen, that were greater in other men's eyes, then in their owne, and that sought the truth rather then their own praise."[44] Sandys's belief in the divinely inspired truth in the fables of Ovid resembles the Authorized Version's translators' faith in the divine truth of holy writ, and their description of their task may stand at the end of our description of his:

> Translation it is that openeth the window, to let in the light; that breaketh the shell, that we may eat the kernel; that putteth aside the curtaine, that we may looke into the most Holy place; that removeth the cover of the well, that wee may come by the water, even as *Jacob* rolled away the stone from the mouth of the well, by which meanes the flockes of *Laban* were watered.

5

Dryden
Translation as Style

It is by now a critical commonplace to remark how much of Dryden's nondramatic poetry consists of translation. "For every line of original nondramatic poetry he wrote two lines of translation from a foreign poet."[1] In this great body of translation, some 38,500 lines, translation from Ovid bulks large. Between 1680 and his death Dryden translated three elegies from the *Amores* (1.1, 1.4, and 2.19), three of the *Heroides* (7, 9, and 16), Book 1 of the *Ars Amatoria*, and two complete books (1 and 12) of the *Metamorphoses*, as well as large parts of six others (8, 9, 10, 11, 13, and 15). Dryden, who had an engaging habit of claiming that whatever author he was reading was nearest to his genius and dearest to his heart, made the same claim for Ovid, and his sympathy with Ovid was used in the next century to explain why his versions of Ovid were more nearly perfect than his Virgil.[2]

Modern critics have not been so quick to single out the Ovid translations for praise. Dryden's treatments of Virgil, Juvenal, and Lucretius have seemed—with reason, I think—to offer more to the reader intent on translation as significant transformation of an original.[3] For us, however, his Ovid translations provide critical opportunities and even demand critical attention. We have already seen that Marlowe's translation of the *Amores* requires reading based on concepts of numerology that now seem arcane and conventions of reading that have been forgotten. Sandys's Ovid, too, for all that it seemed to later readers to be a product of the same attitude toward translation as that which produced

Pope's *Iliad*, proved to be rooted in Renaissance attitudes toward poetry and truth which Pope, although he would have recognized them, might have understood in very different ways.[4] By setting Dryden's handling of Ovid against his predecessors' (and especially Sandys's, which he often imitates), we will be able to see how ideas of translation and the translator's function change between Sandys and Dryden. Dryden's own remarks on Ovid and translation will help. Dryden was a better translator than most critics and a better critic than most translators, and few translators have been as generous or as able in revealing the premises of their translations.

In the preface to *Fables Ancient and Modern*, the last collection of his translations to be published in his lifetime, Dryden passed judgment on his greatest predecessor in translating Ovid:

> I hope I have translated them [sc., the stories from the *Metamorphoses*] closely enough, and given them the same turn of verse which they had in the original; and this, I may say, without vanity, is not the talent of every poet. He who has arrived the nearest to it, is the ingenious and learned Sandys, the best versifier of the former age. . . .[5]

By 1700 Dryden had found time to reread Sandys. Seven years earlier in the dedication to *Examen Poeticum*, his judgment had been less favorable: Sandys had found Ovid verse, and left him prose. But this assessment was, as Dryden candidly admits, based on memory, and old memory at that: "This at least is the idea which I have remaining of his translation; for I never read him since I was a boy."[6] He goes on to wonder what becomes of Ovid's poetry in Sandys's version, and suggests that all or most of it has evaporated. This fault he lays to the wrong judgment of the age in which Sandys lived: "They neither knew good verse, nor loved it; they were scholars, 'tis true, but they were pedants; and for a just reward of their pedantic pains, all their translations want to be translated into English."

Three things attract our attention in these two passages. First, there is the assumption, on which both contrasting judgments of Sandys are based, that a good translator will be a good versifier, one whose verses will have the same "turn" that they had in the original. Second, there is the assumption that Sandys belongs to a former age, one whose canons of poetry were, whether better or worse, at least different from those of Dryden's own time. In the preface to the *Fables* Dryden reveals his sense of how near in time, and yet how far in spirit, Sandys's age was. Speaking of the "former age," he wonders "if I may properly call it by that name, which was the former part of this concluding century."[7] Finally, there is in Dryden's remarks on Sandys a misunderstanding of the poetic premises of this former age. I have already suggested that Sandys's high reputation in the two centuries that followed him was based on virtues his translation happened to have, rather than on those that he thought of as primary in translating. From Sandys's own point of view, he receives the right reputation for the wrong reason. Dryden illustrates the point. Praising Sandys for the versification which the older translator saw as a secondary quality of his work, an attempt to imitate the smoothness of Ovid's verse because Ovid preserved truth and verse conveyed it, Dryden ignores or dismisses as pedantic the whole system of allegories, correspondences, and divinely inspired ancient truths on which Sandys's choice and presentation of Ovid was, as we have seen, based.

These three observations about Dryden's remarks on Sandys can be attributed to a twofold cause: First, there was a general revaluation, in the half a century separating Sandys's *Metamorphosis* from the first publication of Dryden's Ovid translations, of style and its relation to the value of literature. To put it briefly, and over-simply: at the end of the sixteenth century style—the writer's disposition of words to achieve effects—was of secondary importance in the theory and conscious practice of literature. In this age, of course, as in any other, writers paid careful attention to style, but they did not believe style to be their most important concern. By the end of the seventeenth century, style had become not only the primary subject of literary theory and criticism but almost the only one.

Second, and of more general import, the world view upon which earlier ideas of the place of style in literature, and much else, had been based collapsed. The rapid advance of the natural sciences, the Civil War and the beheading of the head of state—an act whose symbolic importance and repercussion in the art and thought of the time should not be underestimated—and the conviction, already mentioned, of people in the seventeenth century that truth was simple and could be known directly, an attitude common to such diverse characters as George Fox, Thomas Hobbes, and Isaac Newton, all contributed to this collapse.

Immediately several cautions and qualifications need to be entered. Generalizations, and especially generalizations that attempt to impose a pattern upon the history of something as subject to personal choices as literary composition, must not be confused with truth. It would be rash to suppose that no one in Sandys's day, or Marlowe's, believed that style deserved the prime place among the virtues of a writer, or to assume that every writer based his work upon the Neoplatonic and Pythagorean doctrines and commonplaces which we found behind Sandys's and Marlowe's translations. Equally, it would be erroneous to suppose that those same ideas were vanished or unintelligible in Dryden's day, or that every writer then looked upon himself as a word-mechanic and nothing more. The situation is far more complicated than this, and writers' practice variable. Translation, furthermore, is a kind of writing in which style is bound to be more important than in original composition, where the substance and arrangement of the work are open to the writer's free choice.

> And by improving what was writ before,
> Invention labours less, and judgment more.

Confining this inquiry to translation may have forced an unbalanced emphasis on style in the later translations and on external dogmas and doctrines in the earlier. Nevertheless, before the Restoration, translation's goal was truth; after the Restoration, translation's goal was style.

We have seen that Sandys's belief in the divine origins of poetry and its essential connection with truth was not unique to him. He left only the briefest comments on the style of his translation and of Ovid, and his general views on the relation of poetry to style had to be deduced with the help of Bacon and Chapman. Several of his contemporaries, however, left more explicit pronouncements on this subject. Three passages, all written at about the time Sandys was translating the *Metamorphoses*, will give an idea of how widespread was the view that style was not the essential element, and how different were the premises of criticism in what Dryden called "the former age" from those of the years after 1660.

Michael Drayton, in his *Epistle to Sir Henry Reynolds, Of Poets and Poesie* (1627), implies an interesting and paradoxical distinction between true poetry and prose, and what only seems to be poetry or prose. Speaking of Nashe, he says, "And surely *Nashe*, though he a Proser were, / A branch of Lawrell yet deserves to beare; / Sharply *Satirick* was he. . . ." In other words, Nashe's subject matter, and the spirit behind it, are enough to qualify him for the title of poet. Samuel Daniel, on the other hand, was "too much *Historian* in verse; / His rimes were smooth, his meeters well did close, / But yet his maner better fitted prose." Smoothness and correctness are not enough to make a poet, for what is in fact prose can take the shape of verse. For Dryden, we recall, a good translator was first of all a good versifier.

On the surface little may seem to separate Drayton's remarks from, say, Matthew Arnold's remark that Dryden and Pope wrote prose in verse. Arnold's implied distinction between genius, inspiration, and authenticity on the one hand, and technique, dullness, and artificiality on the other, grew as the eighteenth century progressed, became an unspoken assumption during the nineteenth, and is not extinct in our own. Like Drayton's remarks, it can trace part of its intellectual ancestry back to Aristotle's distinction between poetry and verse at *Poetics* 1447b, and part to Horace's comparison of Ennius and Lucilius at *Sermones* 1.4, 56–62:

> his, ego quae nunc
> olim quae scripsit Lucilius, eripias si
> tempora certa modosque, et quod prius ordine verbum est
> posterius facias, praeponens ultima primis,
> non, ut si solvas "postquam Discordia taetra
> Belli ferratos postis portasque refregit,"
> invenias etiam disiecti membra poetae.*

---

* Take regular meter, rhythm from my verses—put Lucilius with 'em and do the same. Word order doesn't matter; last first, first last, like prose. But when you shatter old Ennius' verse, about how "Discord's din War's posts and brazen gates had broken in," you'll recognize the Poet, even sundered.

Aristotle we shall come to in a moment. Horace is talking about two different kinds of diction in poetry, not about true, authentic poetry and false, artificial poetry, or about poetry and something else. Drayton, on the other hand, is distinguishing poetry, which may have the external appearance of prose, from something else: prose, will still be prose even if it takes the form of technically perfect verse.

What Drayton meant, or rather assumed, becomes clear when we examine another use of Horace's figure of the dismembered poet, this time in Sir William Alexander's *Anacrisis, or a Censure of Some Poets Ancient and Modern*, written probably in 1634.[8]

> Language is but the Apparel of Poesy, which may give Beauty, but no Strength: And when I censure any Poet, I first dissolve the general Contexture of his Work in several Pieces, to see what Sinews it hath, and to mark what will remain behind, when that external Gorgeousness, consisting in the Choice or Placing of Words, as if it would bribe the Ear to corrupt the Judgment, is first removed, or at least only marshalled in its own Degree. I value Language as a Conduit, the Variety thereof to several Shapes, and adorned Truth or witty Inventions that which it should deliver.

True poetry, that is, is true not because it proceeds from an especially valid or authenticating experience, or because it consists of words disposed in one way as against another, but because it conveys truth. Writing that does not convey truth may be beautiful, but it will not be poetry. Style—"the Choice or Placing of Words"—may be stripped away without impairing the essential nature of poetry. Versification, rhetoric, the art of fashioning a line, the "turn of verse" that Dryden sought in his translations— all are peripheral to poetry itself.

Since Sandys shared this view, it is not surprising that he says so little about the choice or placing of words in the apparatus of his 1632 *Metamorphosis*. Had he wanted to comment on them, of course, the vocabulary was there, but to those who shared his view of poetry such matters were outside their concern. Also in 1632 Drayton's friend Henry Reynolds published his *Mytho-*

mystes, "the chief example in English of the systematic application of Neoplatonism to the interpretation of poetry."[9] He warns his readers not to expect either stylish discussion or discussion of style and informs us what system of terminology was available to him had he cared to consider style:

> Look not, generous Reader (for such I write to), for more in the few following leaves then a plaine and simple verity, unadorned at all with eloquution or Rhetoricall phrase, glosses fitter perhaps to be set upon silken and thinne paradoxical semblances, then appertaining to the care of who desires to lay downe a naked & unmasked Trueth. Nor expect here an Encomium or praise of any such thing as the world ordinarily takes Poesy for: That same thing beeing, as I conceive, a superficiall meere outside of Sence, or gaye barke only (without the body) of Reason.[10]

The next few paragraphs give examples of the "gaye barke" and make it clear that for Reynolds style was equivalent to the traditional art of rhetoric. Its elaborate system of technical terminology provided the critic with means of discussing style, just as it provided the writer with means of adorning thought. But Reynolds believed that the devices of rhetoric were external to the meaning of a piece of poetry. The division between form and content was absolute, and the formal element in poetry was "a superficiall meere outside" of its essential element: "Sence," "Reason," or "Trueth."

Drayton, Alexander, and Reynolds do not stand alone in advocating the idea that poetry is essentially true discourse. Their view in one form or another was common in the late sixteenth and early seventeenth century, as common as the analogic, Neoplatonic world view on which it was in most cases based. Not everyone, of course, saw poetry in this way, nor were all poems or even all translations made by applying the devices of rhetoric or versification to the writer's idea of truth. It would be difficult, for example, to extract a core of Neoplatonic truth from a fundamentally political translation like Thomas May's Lucan, or from such lyric adaptations of antiquity as Jonson's *To Celia*. Nor are Neoplatonic doctrines the only background to Renaissance criticism. Besides the Hermetic and Pythagorean notions that were closely associated with Neoplatonism, Aristotle has a role to play.

In one sense, of course, poetry always claims to be true discourse. Poets hardly ever set out to tell lies; in every age they assert the essential truth of what they do. But a distinction can be drawn between the basically Neoplatonic view of Sandys, Bacon, Drayton, Alexander, Reynolds, and others that poetry's value comes from the truth it conveys, and the common eighteenth-century view, based for the most part on Aristotle and Horace, that poetry's value comes from the way it conveys truth. To the Renaissance critic, the form of poetry, its shape as verse, was secondary to its nature as imitation of an ideal; as Sidney put it, "it is not ryming and versing that maketh a Poet, no more than a long gown maketh an advocate."[11] For this subordination of form to mimetic purpose the critic had the authority of Aristotle, who had distinguished poets from writers of verse and pointed out that Homer and Empedocles, for example, have nothing in common but meter.[12] But Renaissance critics, under the influence of Neoplatonic thought, tended to emphasize Aristotle's statement that the poet must imitate things as they ought to be over his statement that the poet might also imitate things as they were or are.[13] Poetry, Aristotle had suggested, differs from history in that poetry deals with the universal, history with the particular;[14] to this the Renaissance critic added that the universal must necessarily be an ideal, and that the value of poetry comes from its connection with this ideal and divine truth. If the critic had Aristotle in mind, he would talk of poetry's imitation of this truth; if he was following the Neoplatonists, he would talk of its derivation from or participation in the truth. In either case, it is the truth that makes the poetry important.

Eighteenth-century critics read their Aristotle, but read him rather differently. For them nature was the only object of poetic mimesis:

First follow *Nature*, and your judgment frame
By her just standard, which is still the same:
Unerring *Nature*, still divinely bright,
One clear, unchang'd, and universal light,
Life, force, and beauty, must to all impart,
At once the source, and end, and test of Art.[15]

And nature was redefined along with Aristotelian mimesis. Nature was now becoming the material nature of modern science and ceasing to be understood as the ideal Nature of the Renaissance Neoplatonists. Eighteenth-century critics could never have accepted, as Sandys would have, Sidney's statement that "Nature never set forth the earth in so rich tapistry as divers Poets have done .... Her world is brazen, the Poets only deliver a golden."[16] In imitating nature, the eighteenth-century poet would be imitating not only things as they were and are but also things as they ought to be. To eighteenth-century criticism, things as they were, are, and ought to be, the three objects mentioned by Aristotle, were aspects of one single object of imitation.

Style, the choice and placing of words, could be seen from two sides in the eighteenth century. On the one hand, style is only the external guise of thought, which ought not to impede understanding of thought's object:

> . . . true Expression, like th' unchanging Sun,
> Clears, and improves whate'er it shines upon,
> It gilds all objects, but it alters none.
> Expression is the dress of thought, and still
> Appears more decent, as more suitable.[17]

On the other hand, style matters very much, for without it understanding of nature, the object of poetry, is difficult or impossible: "True Wit is Nature to advantage dress'd." Hence poetry must be judged not only by the standard of decorum, which it shares with all mimetic arts, but first by the standard of style, and in particular of the style peculiar to it: "But most by Numbers judge a Poet's song." The new importance of style in post-Restoration literary criticism grew out of the developing understanding that a certain kind of style was what distinguished poetry from the other arts, and that style—"true Expression," in the passage just quoted—could be distinguished from the tricks and adornments of rhetoric.

We are reminded from time to time that ideas have no history, and it may be futile to attempt to trace the separate paths of Neoplatonic, Hermetic, Pythagorean, or Aristotelian elements in Renaissance literary criticism. What must be emphasized, however, is how completely the view of poetry put forward by critics like Drayton, Alexander, and Reynolds, by Sidney before them, and by Sandys in his monumental Ovid of 1632 held the field in criticism. This Neoplatonic theory of poetry grew up in England not as a reaction to any other coherent theory of literature but as a response of serious thinkers to what they saw as abuse and trivialization of literature. It is part of, and in its earliest occurrences prefigures, the general desire to know God's truth directly which lies behind so much of the intellectual, political, and social life of late-Renaissance England. Bacon, for example, is not putting forward an alternative theory when he comes to discuss style in Book One of the *Advancement of Learning*; he is correcting an abuse which, as he saw it, grew up after the Reformation from four causes: "the admiration of ancient authors, the hate of the Schoolemen, the exact studie of languages, and the efficacie of Preaching."[18] All these brought about "an affectionate studie of eloquence and copie of speech." Bacon regarded the system of rhetoric not as a theory of literature but rather as a disorder of language: "Here then is the first distemper of learning, when men studie words and not matter." In the second book he analyzes the meaning of "Poesie" and dismisses its stylistic aspect as of secondary importance, a mere craft or technical skill.

> [Poesie] is taken in two senses, in respect of Words or Matter. In the first sense it is but a *Character* of stile, and belongeth to Arts of speeche, and is not pertinent for the present. In the later, it is, as hath beene saide, one of the principall Portions of Learning, and is nothing else but FAINED HISTORY, which may be stiled as well in Prose as in Verse.[19]

Systematic rhetoric, the "Arts of speeche," which had been the dominant tool of reading in antiquity, offered no serious challenge to the basically Neoplatonic theory of Renaissance criticism in England. Rhetoric's practical function and its descriptive, analytic nature kept it in a secondary position during an age when most men's thoughts were directed by, and found expression in, systems of analogy and synthesis. As for Aristotelian and Horatian definitions of poetry as essentially mimetic, they were given a Neoplatonic coloring in their use by Renaissance critics, and it is difficult to separate these ideas from their Neoplatonic matrix.

The ideas of Sandys and the others had no serious rival as a theory of poetry until the age of Dryden, and their predominance is what confronted him when he looked at the generation of his grandparents and found it a former age, full of poets who "neither knew good verse, nor loved it," who were scholars but pedants.

Dryden, then, beginning to translate Ovid, looked back on the translations of a former age: Sandys and Golding for the *Metamorphoses*; Turberville, Wye Saltonstall (1636), and John Sherburne (1639) for the Heroides; Thomas Heywood (1600?), Francis Wolferston (1661), and Thomas Hoy (1622) for the *Ars Amatoria*; an anonymous translation of 1683, and perhaps Marlowe, for the *Amores*.[20] Most of these seemed to him products of a remote age whose versification was crude and whose ideas of literature pedantic and fanciful. As he saw it, style was the important thing in translating, the mark by which a translator plotted his course and the standard by which he should be judged. Dryden's observation of a change in literary sensibility and theories between his day and Sandys's compels us to ask why the change took place.

Philosophers might say that the change was over-determined. It hardly needs saying that the seventeenth century was a time of change and upheaval in every aspect of English society. Some young man who had bought a crisp new copy of Sandys's *Metamorphosis* in 1632 would have had good reason to feel, as his shaking hand turned over the pages of the book in 1682, that the old volume's commentary belonged to an age so remote as to be unrecognizable, even if he had taken no notice of developments in poetry and literary criticism and had read scarcely a word of Dryden. To work out the political and social causes of literary change during the seventeenth century, their mutual influences and interactions, is beyond my powers and outside the scope of this book.

About one cause, however, we can be somewhat less vague. The new perception of style and its importance in translation can be traced to a more widespread intellectual phenomenon, the rise of neoclassicism. The Restoration brought back not only an exiled king but also numbers of Englishmen whose time on the Continent had been spent in the study or absorption of French manners and ideas. It has been easy to exaggerate the influence of French neoclassicism on its English counterpart, and to forget that the doctrines of Corneille and Boileau fell upon ground prepared to receive them. The analogy between Augustan Rome and Charles II's England, which in one form or another is fundamental to English neoclassicism, finds its first clear expression in *Astraea Redux*, but Waller had used a similar analogy between Augustus and Cromwell in his "Panegyric to my Lord Protector."[21] Nevertheless, French critical theory was the catalyst of an English reaction against the poetic theories and, to some extent, the practices of the preceding age. The advances, also, in critical understanding of antiquity made by the Scaligers, Vossius, the two Casaubons, and other northern European scholars helped to demolish the unhistorical view of antiquity that had been an integral part of the Neoplatonic Renaissance theory of poetry advanced by Bacon, Sandys, and others. When in 1614 Isaac Casaubon accurately dated the *Hermetica*, to give but one example, it was no longer possible for the learned world to rely on the fruitful but mistaken belief that those treatises preserved an Egyptian wisdom older than the Greeks. Those who did ignore Casaubon's redating, like Robert Fludd and Athanasius Kircher, increasingly appear lost in a cul-de-sac of learning.[22] Dryden's expressed scorn for pedantic Dutch commentators in the prefaces to *Sylvae* and to *Ovid's Epistles* represents a waning of their influence, not a refutation of their importance.[23]

The importation and development of neoclassical ideas about literature and the newly accurate knowledge of antiquity made inevitable an increasing emphasis on style in translation. To see how this came about, we must look for a moment at the nature of Dryden's neoclassicism and how it differs from the Neoplatonic world view of Sandys and from the Renaissance neoclassicism of Ben Jonson.

Analogy is fundamental to neoclassicism. Writing, like every other department of life, must be measured against its analogue in classical antiquity:

Ask no advice, but think alone,
Suppose the Question not your own:
How would I act? is not the Case,
How would *Brutus* in my Place?

In such a Case would *Cato* bleed?
And how would *Socrates* proceed?[24]

Augustus and Charles II, Rome and London, ancient tragedy and modern—the practice of analogy bore fruit on most branches of the arts and led in developed neoclassicism to the view that the idea of Greco-Roman antiquity constituted a complete world totally applicable to the contemporary world. The analogy became perfect. Although neoclassicism was not an exclusively literary phenomenon, it was natural that antiquity should be seen largely through the remains of its literature. In Dryden's lifetime especially, scientific archaeology and the study and making available of antiquity's physical remains by the dilettanti and the great nineteenth-century collectors were far in the future. The total world of antiquity had to be sought first in its literature.[25]

Since life was to be grounded in an analogy between modern times and an antiquity preserved in literature and lived as an imitation of this largely literary antiquity, purely literary qualities assumed an importance they had not formerly had. Style became a matter of first importance, and the judgment of style, criticism, became one of the most important duties of the man who would live rightly. Rules of style seemed to have the force of ethical precepts. Translation too assumed a new importance. It was, for one thing, the most direct way of imitating ancient literature, whether one chose, to use Dryden's categories, the "servile path" of literal translation, the "libertine way" of free imitation, or some middle, and in Dryden's view therefore essentially classical, way.[26] For another, translation could be seen as a metaphor for the cultural development of which neoclassicism saw itself as the culmination. To translate Ovid into English was the same as making him speak English or become an Englishman. It was to appropriate him for English letters. "The noblest Fruits, Transplanted, in our Isle / With early Hope and fragrant Blossoms smile."[27]

Neoclassicism is based on an analogy, but so is Neoplatonism. What happens with or around the Restoration is that the place of ultimate reality in the analogy undergoes a shift. Because men wanted to know the truth directly, they placed truth where it could be so known: in our world, the world of the senses.

Hobbes's empiricism and Dryden's neoclassicism are equally part of this relocation of truth. The analogy between macrocosm and microcosm and between the ideal world and the world of the senses came to be replaced by an equally potent analogy between the ancient world and the modern. In this new analogy, accessible truth was shifted away from an ideal world or a world remote from human history to a world that was, though remote in time, of the same order of reality as our own. Writing from the old analogy, Bacon could hope for a partial restoration of an Adamic and perfect correspondence between Word and World; Dryden could use the new analogy to propose that words were our only means of reproducing the perfection of the classical world. Neo-classicism attempted to see things in the light of reason; it is equally true that Neoplatonism attempted to see reason by the light of things.

The contrast between Dryden and Sandys (and, it needs to be said once more, between the Augustan age and the late Renaissance in English literature) is the contrast between literature conceived as means and literature conceived as end. In the Neoplatonic thought of the late Renaissance, literature was a phenomenon of this world, a hypostasis of ideal poesy, and hence essentially unreal. Further, an actual poem, the words on the page and in the mouth, insofar as it described the world known to the senses, was a projection of a projection and doubly unreal. A translation of a poem ran the risk of losing touch with reality altogether unless, like Du Bartas, Sandys, and in a rather different way Marlowe, it claimed connection through divine poesy with that ideal reality from which it was so remote. Style, therefore, did not matter. In neoclassical thought, literature belonged to the same world as the ideal to which it aspired. The historical process of, to use a metaphor employed by Dryden, translation of learning from Greece and Rome to Restoration England was also the process of realization of an ideal of literature. Style, therefore, mattered very much, for it was the means to and measure of an ideal. Truth in the neoclassical schema is still something apart from aesthetics. It is to be sought in the order manifest in "nature, and nature's God," and poetry derives its moral value from its expression of this truth. But neoclassical truth is closer to the world of aesthetic experience than Neoplatonic truth and takes us a step nearer to the belief that truth is beauty and beauty, truth.

It is for this reason that Dryden's neoclassicism is very different from Ben Jonson's. Jonson's neoclassicism, as he tells us in *Timber, or Discoveries*, was based on the old analogy. Poetry in Jonson's view, as in Bacon's and Sandys's, originated with God and passed from Him to us through the Mosaic and Greco-Roman tradition:

> Now, the Poesy is the habit or the Art; nay, rather the Queene of Arts, which had her Originall from heaven, received thence from the *'Ebrewes*, and had in prime estimation with the *Greeks*, transmitted to the *Latines* and all Nations that profess'd Civility.[28]

Because poetry had a divine origin, poets sought truth before style. The poet was to be an imitator, not of Greek and Latin literature for its own sake but of the truth which was to be found in that literature about man and his world.

> A *Poet* is that which by the *Greeks* is call'd $\kappa\alpha\tau$ $\dot{\epsilon}\xi o\chi\dot{\eta}\nu$ $\dot{o}$ $\Pi o\iota\eta\tau\dot{\eta}s$, a Maker, or a fainer: His art, an Art of imitation or faining, expressing the life of man in fit measure, numbers, and harmony, according to Aristotle: From the word $\pi o\iota\hat{\epsilon}\iota\nu$, which signifies to make or fayne. Hence he is call'd a *Poet*, not hee which writeth in measure only, but that fayneth and formeth a fable, and writes things like the Truth. For the Fable and Fiction is, as it were, the forme and Soule of any Poeticall worke or *Poeme*.[29]

Jonson's ideal poetry as much as Drayton's or Alexander's depended very little on style. Content, not form, defined poetry. Dryden, in contrast, believed in the defining power of style.

The use of translation as a metaphor for the progress of arts and letters, and the correlative emphasis on literary style as indication and test of civilized values, runs through Dryden's poem "To the Earl of Roscommon, on his Excellent *Essay on Translated Verse*."[30] Roscommon had traced the history of translation and singled out translators as the keepers of classical virtue in its purest form. Addressing them, he says (lines 7–13),

But since the *Press*, the *Pulpit*, and the *Stage*

Conspire to censure and expose our Age,
Provok'd too far, we resolutely must
To the few Vertus that we have be just.
For who have long'd, or who have labour'd more
To search the Treasures of the *Roman* store,
Or dig in *Grecian Mines* for *purer Oar?*

Dryden takes up Roscommon's suggestion and gives a history of translation in which the progress of style, the progress of translation, and the progress of civilization become one. He begins by rejecting as unprovable any assertion that Egyptian or Near Eastern learning are more ancient, and therefore more true, than the learning of the Greeks.

Whether the fruitful Nile, or Tyrian shore
The seeds of art and infant science bore,
'Tis sure the noble plant, translated first,
Advanced its head in Grecian gardens nursed.

Dryden has expanded Roscommon's image of translation as transplantation into a picture of all art and science as gardening.[31] In an expansion of category that seems to anticipate the translation-centered linguistic philosophy of twentieth-century critics like George Steiner and Walter Benjamin, he establishes translation as the central activity in the garden of culture. It is translation not merely as transfer from language to language but as transfer from culture to culture that allows arts and sciences to find soil in which they will flourish.

Although translation in Dryden's extended sense may not be exclusively literary, it is inextricably linked to literature, and specifically to poetry:

The Grecians added verse; their tuneful tongue
Made nature first, and nature's God their song.
Nor stopped translation here: for conquering Rome
With Grecians' spoils brought Grecian numbers home;
Enrich'd by those Athenian Muses more
Than all the vanquish'd world could yield before.

The literature of Greco-Roman civilization, and not the Hermetic or antediluvian doctrines sought by Sandys, represents for Dryden the point of highest achievement to which subsequent cultures should aspire. Greek literature was first in quality as it was first in time because to the inchoate musings of previous Egyptian and Near Eastern cultures it added verse, and this "tuneful tongue" and ordered utterance gave to that literature the power of imitation of ordered nature, and thereby of the God of which nature is the visible manifestation.

After the glories of Greco-Roman literature, which were as near to perfect imitation of nature as mortals could hope to reach, Dryden saw debasement of both culture and verse. "Barb'rous nations, and more barb'rous times / Debas'd the majesty of verse to rhymes," and even the poets of the Italian Renaissance "Restor'd a silver, not a golden age." Only in the England of Charles II was there a threefold restoration: of the king himself; of the classical, civilized values of Greece and Rome; and of the crucial art of translation, set forth in Roscommon's *Essay*.

> The wit of Greece, the gravity of Rome
> Appear exalted in the British loom;
> The Muses' empire is restored again
> In Charles his reign, and by Roscommon's pen.

The claim that an *Essay on Translated Verse* could restore the lost perfection of the classical civilizations would seen audacious and implausible if Dryden had not prepared us to accept it by equating the progress of translation with the progress of literature, literature with civilization and order, and order with nature and nature's God.

This restored and restoring translation is for Dryden a matter of style. Its decline from the first perfection of Greek and Roman literature was not a lapse from a state of perfect human knowledge like the state which Bacon posited, but a lapse from perfection of style into barbarity. Any improvement in knowledge must also be an improvement in style:

> But Italy, reviving from the trance
> Of Vandal, Goth, and monkish ignorance,
> With pauses, cadence, and well vowell'd words,
> And all the graces a good ear affords,
> Made rhyme an art.

The contrast of Dryden's conception of the progress of human knowledge with Bacon's can best be seen in the contrast between the two men's ideas of the place of style—"pauses, cadence, and well vowell'd words"—in this progress. Dryden, as we can see not only from "To the Earl of Roscommon" but from his other critical writing as well, believed that style was the test of a work of literature and that literature was central to the neoclassical ideal against which human progress was to be measured. Hence style became the standard and goal of the progress of human knowledge. Bacon, on the other hand, held a view of style essentially similar to that represented by Sandys, Drayton, Reynolds, and Alexander. As the discussion of the two meanings of "Poesie" from the *Advancement of Learning* shows, style was for Bacon equivalent to rhetoric, the "Arts of speeche," and not relevant to poesy considered as one of the principal divisions of learning. Style, in fact, was indifferent to this poesy, which could "be stiled as well in Prose as in Verse."[32]

After tracing the history of poetry and civilization down to the second perfection of style "In Charles his reign, and by Roscommon's pen," Dryden turns to Roscommon himself and his poem. He praises the *Essay* for its "needful rules" and compliments its author on his own translations. This combination of theory and practice recreates in one man the roles of the two pattern-figures of Augustan neoclassicism: "Scarce his own Horace could such rules ordain, / Or his own Virgil sing a nobler strain." Further, the Anglo-Irish Roscommon unites in himself two other strains of culture:

> How much in him may rising Ireland boast,
> How much in gaining him has Britain lost!
> Their island in revenge has ours reclaimed,
> The more instructed we, the more we still are sham'd
> 'Tis well for us his generous blood did flow,
> Derived from British channels long ago;
> That here his conquering ancestors were nursed;
> And Ireland but translated England first.

Roscommon himself becomes a translation, a moment in which the relation of one culture to another and the progress of civilization crystallize into real words or real flesh.

This bold extension of an already extended sense of "translation" prepares us for the last sixteen lines of the poem, in which Dryden uses a complex pattern of classical allusions to establish his position in the world which he has set up of progress by translation. After praising the translation of Ovid by the Earl of Mulgrave, whose *Art of Poetry* Roscommon had lauded at the beginning of his essay, Dryden continues:

> When these translate, and teach translators too,
> Nor firstling kid, nor any vulgar vow
> Should at Apollo's grateful altar stand;
> Roscommon writes, to that auspicious hand,
> Muse feed the bull that spurns the yellow sand.

As the California edition points out, these lines are meant to recall the lines in praise of Pollio from Virgil's Third *Eclogue*:

> *Damoetas*: Pollio amat nostram, quamvis est rustica,
>   Musam:
>   Pierides, vitulam lectori pascite vestro.
> *Menalcas*: Pollio et ipse facit nova carmina: pascite taurum,
>   iam cornu petat et pedibus qui spargat harenam.[33]

The allusion suggests that Dryden's muse raises a sacrifice to Roscommon as the English equivalent of Gaius Asinius Pollio, the Roman general, critic, historian, and patron of letters. Dryden, in this Virgilian context, will become the English Virgil, embodiment of the work he would later translate, just as Roscommon earlier had been presented as a translation from Ireland to England, an embodiment both of the art which his essay illuminated and of the progress of civilization as translation which his *Essay* advanced.

Finally, Dryden completes his neoclassical analogy by breaking free of it. The English Augustans are to follow Roscommon's injunction to "be, what Rome or Athens were before," and

> On equal terms with ancient wit engage,
> Nor mighty Homer fear, nor sacred Virgil's page:
> Our English palace open wide in state;
> And without stooping they may pass the gate.

The gate recalls that of Evander's palace at *Aeneid* 8.359–69, and also the metaphorical temple of fame erected by Virgil at

Georgics 3.13–48. Dryden, England's new Virgil, inspired by England's new Pollio, Roscommon (who has suddenly been relegated from the foreground which he had occupied in the early part of the poem), will produce "the greatest work which the soul of man is capable to perform," an epic poem to rival those of classical antiquity. Dryden no doubt means the English epic which he had proposed eight years earlier in the prologue to *Aureng-Zebe*,[34] but it was with his translation of Virgil that he finally fulfilled his ambition for epic. This was fitting enough, for in "To the Earl of Roscommon" he presents the progress of civilization as an act of translation and himself as Virgil translated.

Style, not truth, defines the worth of a translation, even in the extended sense which Dryden sets forth in "To the Earl of Roscommon." To see how far Dryden was from the truth-based valuation of translation which he saw, and failed to understand, in the "former age" of Sandys, we need only look at the way he handles Chapman's remarks on freedom and literalness in translating. In his remarks "To the Reader" prefaced to his *Iliads* of 1616, Chapman had rejected excessively literal translators. The other extreme is to him no better.

> I laugh to see [literal translators]—and yet as much abhorre
> More licence from the words than may expresse
> Their full compression and make clear the Author.
>   From whose truth if you think my feet digresse
> Read Valla, Hessus, and other commentators,
>   And see that my conversion much abates
> The licence they take, and much more showes him too,
>   Whose right not all those great learn'd men have done
> (In some maine parts) that were his Commentars.

The value of Homer, and the quality which a translator ought to preserve above all others, is his truth. Chapman believes that his translation conveys this truth better even than all the works of learned commentators. The reason for this is that the commentators, like the too faithful or too free translators, lack the essential tool by which truth is found.

> But (as the illustration of the Sunne)
>   Should be attempted by the erring starres)

They failed to search his deep and treasurous hart.
    The cause was that they wanted the fit key
Of Nature, in their down-right strength of Art,
        With Poesie to open Poesie—
Which in my Poeme of the Mysteries
    Revealed in Homer I will clearly prove.

Chapman's "Poesie," like Sandys's, is the divine instrument by which men can know truth and is far removed from Dryden's identification of the progress of civilization with the progress of a poetry defined by style.

It is characteristic of Dryden that he should have missed Chapman's point.

> I remember not the reason why he [Chapman] gives for it [sc., preferring paraphrastical translation]: But I suppose it is, for fear of omitting any of his Excellencies: sure I am, that if it be a fault, 'tis much more pardonable, than that of those, who run into the other extream, of a litteral, and close Translation, where the Poet if confin'd so streightly to his Author's Words, that he wants elbow-room, to express his Elegancies.[35]

It is characteristic, too, that the excellencies of the second clause should have become elegancies by the end of the sentence.

6

Dryden
Style in Translation

Dryden found truth in style. He saw translation as an act of verbal mimesis by which an author's essential qualities could be carried over from one language to another. Translation also, as he asserts in "To the Earl of Roscommon," was a paradigmatic act of neoclassicism. Translation was a metaphor not only for the progress of civilization, but also for that neoclassical procedure of analogy and imitation through which the entire, whole, and perfect pattern of antiquity is recovered and renewed in our own persons and actions. Because the seventeenth century knew classical antiquity largely through its literary remains, neoclassical translation inevitably began with language and style:

> No man is capable of translating poetry who, besides a genius to that art, is not a master both of his author's language and his own. Nor must we understand the language only of the poet, but his particular turn of thoughts and of expression, which are the characters that distinguish and, as it were, individuate him from all other writers.

Only when this technical analysis and mastery has been completed can the translator move on to achieve that identification with his author which will produce a successful translation:

> When we are come thus far, 'tis time to look into ourselves to conform our genius to his, to give his thought either the same turn, if our tongue will bear it, or, if not, to vary but the dress, not to alter or destroy the sub-

stance. . . . By this means the spirit of an author may be transfused, and yet not lost.[1]

Dryden stops short of defining translation as an entirely stylistic art. Unlike twentieth-century critics, whose conceptual universes tend to be not merely centered on language but concerned exclusively with language, Dryden saw content as separable from form, thought from language, judgment from fancy, nature from art. The fact remains, however, that for Dryden, in theory and in practice, translation was the most direct way to recover the classical world, and translation was first of all a matter of style.

Dryden's attitude toward style in translation means that our treatment of him here will differ in several ways from our treatment of Sandys and Marlowe. With those two authors we were concerned to discover ways in which their ideas of translation and its possible functions might affect our reading of the translations they made. Marlowe's version of the *Amores* proved to be a translation whose stylistic defects grew out of the contemporary conventions of reading and numerology which he exploited. Sandys, when we examined him in his self-stated posture as a careful student of Bacon and read his commentary as an integral part of his text, proved to be an author whose stylistic virtues, the very qualities for which he has been admired, were secondary to his main design: to present in English the truth, more ancient than Greece and Rome, which Ovid conveyed. In each case our reading and the translator's design were shaped by an external referent.

Of course, in reading Dryden's translations we are acutely conscious of ways in which his attitude toward his original varies from that which is usual with us. Neoclassicism attributes to the classical texts a prescriptive force which they can never have in our time. Nevertheless, in one respect at least our attitude toward those texts resembles Dryden's. As he did, we think of a translation as an artifact of style, and our standards for judging a translation are almost exclusively stylistic. That this is so testifies to the authority and persuasiveness of Dryden's criticism; he focused the attention of succeeding generations on style in translation, and by doing so he ensured that the metastylistic aims of pre-Restoration translations would be lost from view. The dominance down to our own time of the Drydenic concept of translation means, too, that in this chapter the reading of Dryden's Ovid translations will seem familiar and the translations themselves less remote than those of Marlowe or Sandys.

But we can still ask, as we did with Marlowe and Sandys, what Dryden's Ovid was, or why Dryden chose to translate Ovid instead of, say, Lucan or Statius. "Men of unbounded imagination, but who often wanted the poise of judgement," he calls these two in *The Author's Apology for Heroic Poetry*.[2] What strikes one immediately when one surveys Dryden's remarks on Ovid in his various prefaces and dedications is how little Dryden's judgment of Ovid varied over the course of his life, and how honest, accurate, and unsentimental that judgment was.

Dryden's Ovid is a poet whose strength is in his way of writing. His verse runs sweetly, smoothly, and easily, and in the kind of verbal manipulation called a "turn" he is one of the principal practitioners, or the principal practitioner. But Dryden knows that Ovid has the defects inherent in these qualities of smoothness and agility. His verse can become monotonous, and his delight in the play of words often leads him to overstep the bounds of good taste. In fact, it is Ovid's unnaturalness, his failure to observe decorum and imitate nature, that makes him inferior to both Chaucer and Virgil.[3]

Dryden's judgment of Ovid is so balanced and so consistent that our respect for his honesty as a critic must increase when we read this appreciation:

> Whether it be the partiality of an old man to his youngest child, I know not; but they appear to me to be the best of all my endeavours in this kind. Perhaps this poet is more easy to be translated than some others whom I have lately attempted; perhaps, too, he was more according to my genius.[4]

Only a man who had read himself as accurately as he read Ovid could have combined clearheaded evaluation with this affectionate fondness and a recognition that, though other authors might be more natural or sublime, none was so near to his heart. We are likely to overvalue those we love; it is to Dryden's credit that he did not overvalue Ovid.

The consistency of Dryden's opinion of Ovid suggests that there is no need to preserve a rigorous chronological order in examining his translations, or to examine them all. My decision to begin with "The First Book of Ovid's *Metamorphoses*," from *Examen Poeticum* of 1693 has been prompted by an observation which, though subjective, seems nevertheless worth recording: this translation seems closer to its original—it reads more like Ovid—than any of Dryden's other Ovid translations. In his version of Apollo's pursuit of Daphne (ll.502–24), for example, Dryden catches exactly the baroque abundance and rhetorical passion of Apollo's speech:

> Swift as the Wind, the Damsel fled away,
> Nor did for these alluring Speeches stay:
> Stay Nymph, he cry'd, I follow not a Foe.
> Thus from the Lyon, trips the trembling Doe;
> Thus from the Wolf the frighten'd lamb removes,
> And from pursuing Faulcons fearful Doves,
> Thou shunn'st a God, and shunn'st a God that loves.
> Ah, lest some thorn shou'd pierce thy tender foot,
> Or thou shou'dst fall in flying my pursuit!
> To sharp uneven ways thy steps decline;
> Abate thy speed, and I will bate of mine.
> Yet think from whom thou dost so rashly fly;
> Nor basely born, nor Shepherd's Swain am I.
> Perhaps thou know'st not my Superior State;
> And from that ignorance, proceeds thy hate.
> Me Claros, Delphos, Tenedos obey,
> These hands the Patareian Scepter sway.
> The King of Gods begot me: What shall be,
> Or is, or ever was, in Fate, I see.
> Mine is th' invention of the charming Lyre;
> Sweet notes, and Heav'nly numbers I inspire.
> Sure is my Bow, unerring is my Dart;
> But ah more deadly his, who pierc'd my Heart.
> Med'cine is mine; what Herbs and Simples grow
> In fields and Forrests all their pow'rs I know;
> And am the great Physician call'd below.
> Alas that Fields and Forrests can afford
> No remedies to heal their Love-sick Lord!

To cure the pains of Love, no Plant avails:
And his own Physick, the Physician fails.

Both poet and translator have at their disposal a poetic diction admirably suited to this kind of artful and artificial discourse. In Ovid, Apollo's speech sounds from the beginning the notes of flight and pursuit. The situation combines the mythological, erotic, and rhetorical in a way that we have come to think of as quintessentially Ovidian.[5] As Apollo pursues Daphne, words chase one another in his speech:

Nympha precor, Penei, mane. Non insequor hostis;
Nympha mane! sic agna lupum, sic cerva leonem,
sic aquilam penna fugiunt trepidante columbae,
hostes quaeque suos: amor est mihi causa sequendi!

The repetitions of *nympha* and *mane*, of *hostis* by *hostes* and *insequor* by *sequendi*, and the anaphora of *sic...sic...sic*, all express and reflect the timeless artificiality of the situation. In a real pursuit, something happens—the pursuer catches his quarry, the quarry escapes. Even in Ovid's models for these lines in *Iliad* 22 and *Aeneid* 12, Achilles and Aeneas catch Hector and Turnus. But Apollo and Daphne are locked forever in pursuit and flight. He will never catch her, and in a striking reversal of the cliche in which the pursued runs faster and the pursuer increases his speed to match, Ovid has his god declare that if Daphne will only slacken her speed, he will do likewise rather than see her injure herself on the rough terrain: *Aspera, qua properas, loca sunt. Moderatius, oro / curre fugamque inhibe moderatius insequor ipse.*

In this situation Ovid's rhetoric becomes a true reflector of the erotic and mythological situation. Just as Echo's echoing of Narcissus's words to her represents through a device of language the psychological relation of the two characters, so in Apollo's speech the repetitions and the fact that the speech is unfinished represent in rhetoric the timeless pursuit which joins Apollo and Daphne. This unconsummated pursuit, in which the two characters are linked as if by an invisible rod, is summed up in the simile which precedes Daphne's metamorphosis into a laurel:

Ut canis in vacuo leporem cum Gallicus arvo
vidit, et hic praedam pedibus petit, ille salutem;

alter inhaesuro similis iam iamque tenere
sperat et extento stringit vestigia rostro;
alter in ambiguo est, an sit comprensus, et ipsis
morsibus eripitur tangentiaque ora relinquit:
sic deus et virgo.

The hound and the hare will never catch one another; nor will the god and the maiden. The hound is always hoping, always on the point of seizing his prey, while the hare is always fearful, so close to being caught that she is not even sure that she has not been caught.

In translating this simile Dryden makes one addition that has the effect of weakening his rendering of Ovid's complex presentation of the situation.

As when the impatient Greyhound slips from far,
Bounds o're the Glebe to course the fearful Hare,
She in her speed, does all her safety lay;
And he with double speed pursues the Prey;
O're-runs her at the siting turn, and licks
His Chops in vain and blows upon the Flix;
She scapes, and for the neighb'ring Covert strives,
And gaining shelter, doubts if yet she lives:
If little things with great we may compare,
Such was the God, and such the flying Fair.

It is no doubt Dryden's instinct for decorum that prompted him to add the qualification about the propriety of comparing small matters with great. More significiant, however, is his alteration of the fate of the hare. Unlike Ovid's prey, frozen in the simile forever on the point of being caught and forever just escaping, Dryden's fugitive animal does find shelter and reflects in tranquility over her narrow escape.

In Ovid mythology and rhetoric combine around a complex truth of erotic psychology: that being in love can be a matter of eternal pursuit as well as of eternal possession. Dryden's change reduces this complexity to a simple narrative of pursuit and escape. Because of the way in which Ovid presents the pursuit and flight of Daphne and Apollo, metamorphosis, the extraord-inary transformation of Daphne into a laurel, becomes the only way to resolve the situation. Neither escape nor capture is a possible ending to the story, for the bond between the two characters is, as Apollo recognizes when he cries out "Abate thy speed, and I will bate of Mine," precisely their roles as pursuer and pursued. Daphne's transformation into the laurel which she always was (δάφνη means "laurel" in Greek) and Apollo's continued association with her allow them to continue as what they were. Metamorphosis is the inevitable ending to Ovid's story. In Dryden's version, however, metamorphosis is only one possible ending; like the hare, Daphne might simply have escaped altogether. Instead of summing up the situation, her transformation continues the narrative. In Dryden, the metamorphosis is fanciful, cleverly told, and an adept end to the narrative; in Ovid, it is all these things and inevitable too.

It is easy enough to see in Dryden's simplification of situation into story yet one more example of his affinity for what Mark Van Doren called the poetry of statement.[6] Or perhaps we should talk about the fundamentally different approaches to narrative practiced by Dryden and Ovid. Whichever explanation we choose, it must take into account Dryden's inability or unwillingness to deal with Ovid's multivalent, ironical, or self-doubting mode of writing. Gifted with great rhetorical resources, facility in composition, and affinity for the erotic and mythological, Dryden was in many ways the ideal translator of Ovid. When we come away dissatisfied from one of his renderings, it is almost always because he has failed to catch the notes of linguistic and logical play or ironic self-reference and questioning of appearance and reality that are seldom far away as we read Ovid.

Places where Dryden has smoothed the multiple facets of Ovid's poetry into a uniform and ordered surface are numerous, but one of the clearest examples is the translation of "Ovid's Elegies, Book Two, Elegy the Nineteenth" which appeared in *Miscellany Poems* of 1684. This translation has been highly praised—and misunderstood. The editors of the California edition, representing critical consensus, stress the uniqueness of this version among Dryden's translations. Dryden's translation of the poem's situation from Augustan Rome to London and his transformation of Ovid's elegiac lover into a Restoration gallant "led him to take extraordinary liberties with the text," especially in the last twenty lines, which constitute "one of the few examples of loose imitation among Dryden's translations."[7] At the same time, Dryden carefully provides "a totally responsible English substitution" by seeing to it that his translation has the same number of lines as its original. The translation "was a kind of tour de force, but lest it appear too calculated, he added two lines of valediction."

Doubts may be ventured. Is the final couplet really sufficient to prevent our awareness of the careful correspondence between length of original and length of translation, and can the care taken to assure that correspondence really be reconciled with a view of the translation as "loose imitation"? In fact, upon examination the much-vaunted imitation turns out to be nothing more than a continuous application of Dryden's premise to each successive example in the poem. If Ovid's lover is a Restoration gallant, then *quod licet et facile est quiquis cupit*(l. 31) will become "him who loves an easie Whetstone Whore," an *ancilla* (l. 41) will become an "Orange-wench," *uxorem stulti siquis amare potest* (l. 40) "The sneaking City Cuckold." Dryden's method of translating has not altered in its essentials since his contributions to *Ovid's Epistles* of 1680; if anything, he has stayed closer to the text in his translation of *Amores* 2.19 than in the earlier work. In both his basic procedure is to translate couplet by couplet—as indeed is almost inevitable in translating Ovid's closed elegiacs—but in the earlier translation he is readier to expand one line of Ovid into several or to rework the order of ideas. The modernizations in the later translation differ only in frequency, not in kind, from such modernizations as Dryden's substitution of "Loovre" for Ovid's *Palatia* at *Metamorphoses* 1.227, his insertion of a reference to the deposed Stuarts in "Piety in Exile mourns" at 1.190, and the Miltonic echoes and Christian coloring that figure so largely throughout his translation of *Metamorphoses* 1.[8]

Dryden's modernizations should not distract us for long from continuing our examination of the way in which he transforms Ovid's complex situations into simple ones. In *Amores* 2.19, a lover addresses the husband of his mistress. This is too easy, he complains; do make *some* effort to guard your wench. Pleasure is more keen when we have to work for it. The lover then addresses his mistress on the same theme before returning in line 37 to the

husband. This summary accounts completely for Dryden's trans-
lation, which presents Ovid's poem as a series of variations of this
theme. It does not, however, account for Ovid's poem. As we read
2.19, we become increasingly aware that the lover's complaint
has an extra dimension. Not only does the lover protest that his
mistress's husband is too complaisant; he also fears that this very
complaisance may have the effect of destroying his love affair.
The irony is twofold. The lover exposes the husband's stupidity
by begging him to do what most lovers complain about, but at
the same time he exposes his own dependence on the husband's
obstruction. *Da*, he begs, *locum nostris materiamque dolis*—"Give
me an occasion and some material for our deceptions." If the
husband does not comply, he fears that he will have to stop loving
the man's wife. *Tamque ego praemoneo: nisi tu servare puellam
incipis, incipiet desinere esse mea* (ll. 47–48). Again he complains:
You put up with things no husband should endure; why, your
complaisance will mean—the end of my affair: *lentus es et pateris
nulli patienda marito; / at mihi concessi finis amoris erit* (ll. 51–52).

As so often in the *Amores*, Ovid here is less interested in love
as revealed in his own emotions than in love as a social and
literary phenomenon. Critics have frequently remarked on the
unreality of Ovid's Corinna in contrast to Catullus's Lesbia or
Tibullus's Delia, and some have wasted their time in speculation
on the elusive lady's identity. In fact, Corinna is a fit object for
Ovid's verse. Like the lover in the *Amores*, Corinna is a constant
whose reality comes only from the situations in which she is
presented to us. Corinna and her lover do all that Roman lovers
should: they make love, pass signals at dinner parties, quarrel,
exchange billets-doux, and so on. The very fact that they do all
these things is enough to cast doubt on the suggestion that either
of them has an extra-literary existence. Surely no couple's life
ever imitated art so completely and perfectly. The *Amores* are
poems about love, not love poems, and in 2.19 Ovid takes a
convention of erotic discourse, the complaint against the jealous
husband, and turns it on its head in order to suggest that social
and literary conventions may be just as important to a love affair
as the actual feelings of the people involved. The lover of 2.19
needs the situation of an elegiac lover in order to be in love; if,
thanks to the husband's complaisance, no doors are shut in his

face, if he cannot sigh and pine, then the whole enterprise becomes joyless and insignificant:

> scilicet infelix numquam prohibebor adire?
> nox mihi sub nullo vindice semper erit?
> nil metaum? per nulla traham suspiria somnos?
> nil facies, cur te iure perisse velim?
> quid mihi cum facili, quid cum lenone marito?
> corrumpit vitio gaudia nostra suo.

Like Apollo and Daphne, the lover and mistress of *Amores* 2.19 find themselves in an erotic situation defined by a dynamic of pursuit and flight.

> Bold lover, never, never can'st thou kiss.
> Though winning near the goal – yet, do not grieve;
> She cannot fade, though thou hast not thy bliss,
> Forever wilt thou love, and she be fair.

Unlike Keats, Ovid in 2.19 speculates on what would happen if the rules were changed: if Apollo were to catch Daphne, the husband leave the door unlatched, the mistress be always available. Is love a matter of feelings or of conventions?

And finally there is a hint, no more, of a third level of irony. In the last couplet Ovid has his lover say to the husband, "Why don't you look for someone else who will take pleasure in your tremendous tolerance? If you enjoy having me as your rival, be obstructive"(*quin alium, quem tanta iuvet patientia quaeris? / me tibi rivalem si iuvat esse, veta*). With this suggestion that the husband may prefer the lover of the poem to any other, Ovid makes us pause to wonder: Can it be that the husband's compliance has the same motive, and the same result, as the jealous vigilance of the conventional cheated husband? Can it be that it is the lover, not the husband, who is being cozened?

Confronted with these multiple ironies, Dryden reduces them to a single tone. His replacement of one persona, the elegiac lover, by another, the Restoration gallant, forced a change in style. The elegiac lover was a figure based on life and literature and drawn from patterns found on the streets of Rome and in Hellenistic poetry. The Restoration gallant too could be found in life, but his literary origins were in the drama. The dramatic antecedents of

Dryden's replacement persona insensibly color his translation of
Amores 2.19. The dramatic qualities of Dryden's style in his
translations of *Ovid's Epistles* have been noted:[9] plain diction, few
ornamental adjectives, closed and grammatically complete
couplets, a fondness for exclamation and interrogation. There is
more: in his translation of 2.19, an attention to surface, to the
readily comprehensible presentation of a single action or state
of mind. As early as 1667 in the "Account of the Ensuing Poem"
prefaced to *Annus Mirabilis* Dryden had commented on the
essentially dramatic quality of Ovid's style:

> Ovid images more often [sc., than Virgil] the movements
> and affections of the mind, either combating between two
> contrary passions, or extremely discomposed by one. His
> words therefore are the least part of his care; for he
> pictures nature in disorder, with which the study and
> choice of words is inconsistent. This is the proper wit of
> dialogue or discourse, and consequently of the drama,
> where all that is said is to be supposed the effect of sudden
> thought; which, though it excludes not the quickness of
> wit in repartees, yet admits not a too curious election of
> words, too frequent allusions, or use of tropes, or in fine,
> anything that shows remoteness of thought or labour in
> the writer.[10]

What Dryden saw as the dramatic character of Ovid's style
imposed itself on his translation of *Amores* 2.19 and made him
eschew not only rhetorical elaboration and figures of speech but
also whatever might hint at more than one level of interpretation.
To have done otherwise would have been to weaken the force
of the gallant's monologue, in which was imaged a mind
discomposed by a single passion.

We can see this most clearly by comparing Dryden's transla-
tion to Ovid in those places where the Latin explicitly suggests
a meaning counter to the general drift of the speaker's words.
The lover has been mocking his mistress's husband by suggesting
that he should observe his wife more carefully. His advice to the
husband is ironical at the first level of irony in the poem. But
in lines 47 and 48 we find an explicit pointer to the second level
of irony. The lover warns the husband that if he does not guard

his wife, she may leave her lover.

> iamque ego praemoneo; nisi tu servare puellam
> incipis, incipiet desinere esse mea.

Dryden's translation of the couplet departs completely from the Latin in the second line and eliminates any suggestion that the lover's position may be endangered by the husband's tolerance:

> Look to thy wife, and leave off thy Conniving,
> I'll be no drudge to any Wittall living.

Similarly, in the penultimate couplet where Ovid has the lover speak of the husband's destroying his pleasure, Dryden merely has his gallant continue his scorn and mockery.

> quid mihi cum facili; quid cum lenone marito?
> corrumpit vitio gaudia nostra suo.

Dryden's departure from the Latin is complete and studied.

> Why art thou then so incorrigibly Civil,
> Doe somewhat I may wish thee at the Devil.

In the last couplet Ovid introduces a hint of a third level of irony:

> quin alium quem tanta iuvet patientia, quaeris?
> me tibi rivalem si iuvat esse, veta!

Dryden continues at the same level of irony that he has maintained throughout the poem:

> For shame be no accomplice in my treason,
> A pimping Husband is too much in reason.

In fact, when Dryden cuts loose from Ovid's text in his translation of *Amores* 2.19, it is always in a place where Ovid has suggested a level of irony deeper than Dryden could achieve within the limits of the simple, dramatic, and uniform tone which he has imposed on the poem.

Now that we have seen what the effects were of Dryden's decision to turn Ovid's elegiac lover into a Restoration gallant and of his perception of Ovid's style as essentially dramatic, it becomes easier to understand why he added this two-line coda to his translation of *Amores* 2.19.

Once more wear horns before I quite forsake her,
In hopes whereof I rest thy Cuckold-maker.

The final couplet, which might have seemed an anomalous addition to a translation so obviously crafted line by line and couplet by couplet in step with the original, can now be seen as an attempt to grasp the multiple ironies of the original before they fade and to convey them in a way compatible with the character of the translation. In Ovid the multiple levels of irony work through the poem, becoming more apparent as we read. The third level, at which the irony turns back on itself as it is suggested that the husband may in fact be guarding his wife by his very complaisance, appears as a hint only in Ovid's final couplet, but we have been prepared for it by the poem's general tone and by the fact that it appears in a collection where complex irony and the undercutting coda are common.[11] Dryden, compelled by his choice of style and mode to pass by Ovid's complex irony, chose instead to present the multiple ironies of his original in sequence. "Before I quite forsake her" jars in Dryden's added couplet: it is in Ovid, but not in the Ovid he has given to us.

If there is another note of irony in Dryden's version, it is in the hypothesis of the translation, in the contrast between the familiar raffishness of the gallant and his classical, and therefore decorous, model in Ovid. This kind of irony is implicit in the analogy between past and present that lies at the heart of neoclassicism. The awareness that juxtaposition of past and present might demean the past rather than elevate the present lies behind the parodies and burlesques that sound so prominently against the stately music of neoclassicism. Parody especially indicates that awareness of style as something detachable from meaning which is one characteristic of the neoclassical view of literature. In its single irony and its dependence on juxtaposition of, rather than analogy between, present and past, Dryden's version of *Amores* 2.19 points toward parody, not imitation.

More than the *Amores*, however, the *Heroides* lent themselves to parody as readily as to emulation. In the same year (1680) that *Ovid's Epistles, Translated by Several Hands* (including Dryden's) was published, someone—possibly Matthew Stevenson—published *The Wits Paraphras'd: or paraphrase upon Paraphrase In a Burlesque on the Several late Translations of Ovid's Epistles*. The work is slight, and coarse. A syphilitic Sappho writes to Phaon, and Canace begins her letter to Macareus by observing, "One hand employs my Pen, alas! / with t'other hand I scratch my A––." Even so, the mere existence of this little work suggests that it was style that was important, not only to Dryden but to his readers. *Wits Paraphras'd* burlesques a style, a manner of treating Ovid, and not Ovid himself. Further, as the emphasis on the key word "paraphrase" in the title shows, the parody is addressed to readers familiar with Dryden's threefold division of styles of translation in the "Preface" to *Ovid's Epistles*.

This being the case, it is worth noting that Dryden's version of the *Heroides* was ripe for parody. The parodist wants a simple target, one whose characteristics can be easily recognized even when distorted. In the style of Dryden's contributions to *Ovid's Epistles* we find a counterpart to the simplification of Ovid's complex irony that distinguished his version of *Amores* 2.19. Dryden simplifies, smooths out, and regularizes Ovid's verse.

This statement requires two qualifications before we can look at Dryden's verse in his translation of the *Heroides*. First, Ovid's versification in the *Heroides* is itself simple, smooth, and regular. To give but one example: of the one hundred thirty-four hexameter lines in *Heroides* 17, Helen to Paris, only four (145, 183, 189, and 241) do not have a major caesura in the fifth position. Of the remaining one hundred thirty hexameters, ninety-eight have this penthemimeral caesura accompanied by a caesura in the seventh position. In other words, 75 percent of the hexameters in *Heroides* 17 conform to the pattern

   Dat mihi Leda Jovem cygno decepta parentem,

or, with a dactyl in the third foot,

   Cum modo me spectas oculis, lascive, protervis.

Second, classical scholars from Lachmann on have from time to time doubted that many of the letters in the *Heroides*, especially 9, 15, and the double letters 16–21, are by Ovid.[12] These doubts are not, however, of much significance to our inquiry. Dryden believed that he was translating Ovid; the important question is, How did he do it?

When he translated Ovid's elegiac couplet, Dryden deliberately limited the metrical variety of his own couplet. The easiest way to see this is to isolate one characteristic, the placement of the caesura, and compare Dryden's handling of it in his *Heroides* translations with his handling of it in his other work. Table A (below) compares the distribution of various types of line in Dryden's version of *Heroides* 17 with the distribution in *Astraea Redux* (1660) and in a group of prologues and epilogues written in or shortly before 1680.

From the figures given for the percentage of each type of line in each sample, it is immediately evident that in translating the *Heroides* Dryden deliberately restricted the variety of his verse. He uses significantly fewer lines of types B and G and rather fewer of type E. He uses significantly more type C lines (almost 58 percent in the translation as against 41 percent and 38 percent in the *Astraea Redux* and prologues).

Dryden restricted his versification, most likely, in response to Ovid's restricted line in the *Heroides*. He attempted, as he said in the preface to a later collection, "to restore Ovid to his native sweetness, easiness, and smoothness; and to give my poetry a kind of cadence and, as we call it, a run of verse, as like the original as the English can come up to the Latin."[13] But when he thus limited the variety of his lines, Dryden left himself with verse that was less varied and supple than its original. Compare, for example, the first ten lines of *Heroides* 17 with their counterpart in Dryden's translation. No couplet in the ten lines of Ovid is metrically identical to any other; in fact, only three lines are identical, the pentameter lines 2, 6, and 10, all of which have a spondaic first half (D = dactyl, S = spondee).

D D D D D S	Nunc oculos tua cum violarit epistula nostros
S S – D D –	Non rescribendi gloria visa levis
D D D S D S	Ausus es hospitii temeratis, advena, sacris
D S – D D –	Legitimam nuptae sollicitare fidem!
D S S D D S	Scilicet idcirco ventosa per aequora vectum
S S – D D –	Excepit portu Taenaris ora suo,
D S S S D S	Nec tibi, diversa quamvis e gente venires,
D D – D D –	Oppositas habuit regia nostra fores,
D D S S D S	Esset ut officii merces iniuria tanta?
S S – D D –	Qui sic intrabas, hospes an hostis erat?

If we took into account the varied disposition of ictus and accent, the impression of variety would be even stronger. In Dryden, on the other hand, five of the ten lines conform to type C described above. Iambic feet predominate; in fact, trochees are substituted for iambs only in line 4.

Type D   When loose Epistles violate Chast Eyes,
     C   She half consents, who silently denies:
     D   How dares a Stranger with designs so vain,
     A   Marriage and Hospitable Right Prophane?
     C   Was it for this, your Fate did shelter find
     C   From swelling Seas and every faithless wind?
     F   (For tho a distant Country brought you forth,
     C   Your usage here was equal to your worth.)
     C   Does this deserve to be rewarded so?
     F   Did you come here a Stranger, or a Foe?

These two ten-line samples may stand for the whole. Dryden, seeking Ovidian smoothness and regularity, set stricter limits on the variety of his verse in his translation than in his original works. But even before he set these limits his verse was constrained by rhyme, by the brevity of the English couplet in contrast with the Latin, and by the tendency, which had developed over the century past, for units of expression to coincide with units of verse. The effect of these constraints and Dryden's own restriction of his verse is to present a version of the *Heroides* in a metrical style that suggests but does not reproduce Ovid. Dryden's couplets move like a rocking horse or pendulum; Ovid's, like a school of fish, wheel and dart from one side of their enclosing structure to the other.

Finally, then, Dryden's way of translating Ovid was shaped by an external idea no less than were Marlowe's and Sandys's. For Dryden, however, the ideal was not the power that might come from manipulation of cosmic number or the truth that might be sought in a past remoter than classical antiquity. For Dryden, the ideal was decorum and naturalness. And unlike Marlowe and Sandys, who saw their ideal in Ovid, Dryden found Ovid wanting in the ideal qualities of poetry:

He is often luxuriant, both in his fancy and expressions;
and, as it has lately been observed, not always natural.

TABLE A

Line Type	Heroides 17		Astraea Redux		Prologues*	
A: caesura after first foot	9,	3%	22,	6.81%	6,	2.32%
Go then and boast in some less haughty place						
B: caesura in second foot	2,	0.77%	8,	2.47%	10,	3.87%
Conclude me, by your own example, lost						
C: caesura after second foot	149,	57.52%	133,	41.17%	98,	37.98%
A guilt there was; but oh that guilt was mine						
D: caesura in third foot	53,	20.46%	64,	19.81%	57,	22.09%
The faith of Strangers is too prone to change						
E: caesura after third foot	35,	13.51%	57,	17.64%	62,	24.03%
Ill-bred then let me be, but not unchaste						
F: caesura in fourth foot	13,	5.01%	24,	7.43%	15,	5.81%
For tho a distant Country brought you forth						
G: caesura after fourth foot	0,	0%	15,	4.64%	10,	3.87%
How Great were then our Charles his Woes, who thus						

*Prologue to *Circe*, and an Epilogue; Epilogue to *Mithridates*; Prologue to *A True Widow*; Prologue at Oxford, 1680; Prologue to *Caesar Borgia*; Prologue to *The Loyal General*; Prologue to the University of Oxford. (*Works* 1:156–65.)

If wit be pleasantry, he has it to excess: but if it be pro-
priety, Lucretius, Horace, and above all Virgil, are his
superiors.[14]

In his translation, as was almost inevitable, Dryden attempted
to help Ovid conform to his ideal poetry. Hence in translating
the episode of Daphne and Apollo, Dryden altered the simile of
hare and hound in which Ovid made explicit the mythic paradox
of timeless pursuit and flight so as to make Ovid's myth conform
to the natural world in which things happen in time. In translat-
ing *Amores* 2.19 Dryden made Ovid's complex irony simple and
chose as analogue for Ovid's elegiac lover a figure, the Restoration
gallant, whose nature made a simple voice the only natural one
for the poem. This pruning of luxuriant fancy has its counterpart
in a pruning of luxuriant expression which is easily visible in
the translations from the *Heroides*, where Dryden chose a uni-
form, decorous style of verse to represent the variety that char-
acterizes even Ovid's simplest elegiacs.

Epilogue
Sweet Ovid's Ghost

Insofar as this is a book about translations of Ovid, Dryden's death makes a natural point at which to end it. As Sandys had done before him, Dryden through his translations and criticism gave the literary public a new reading and a new valuation of Ovid. Sandys's revaluation had enabled Ovid to appeal to the new desire to know the truth simply and directly that was a feature of mid-seventeenth-century English intellectual life, and the style in which Sandys presented his truthful Ovid was one whose potential was seen almost immediately by poets and versifiers of his century and the next—though Sandys might not have understood or endorsed the sense of the supreme importance of style that lay behind their approval. Sandys, in fact, created an Ovid who could survive the change in taste that separates the age of Milton from the age of Spenser.

Dryden created an Ovid too frivolous for poets and too indecorous for critics, an author whose future was to be read by schoolboys and remembered, vaguely, by adults. Dryden's judgment of Ovid—that he is an author smooth but monotonous, one who failed to observe decorum and imitate nature, inferior to both Chaucer and Virgil—established the idea of Ovid that was to appear again and again in Augustan criticism. Oxford's Professors of Poetry can always be relied upon not to step too far ahead of the critical consensus of their age, and the first holder of that chair, Joseph Trapp, was no exception. In the English translation, published in 1742, of the lectures given during his term of office, 1711–1719, he summed up Ovid in terms reminiscent of Dryden.

Ovid can move the passions, but

> ...when he does best, he often falls short of that sub-
> limity in which he was naturally deficient; that when
> he shines most, he generally abounds with an unhappy
> luxuriancy of thought, disagreeable repetitions, unseason-
> able and absurd conceits; that his style is loose and
> incorrect. However, let him have his due praise, let him
> be allowed to draw the outlines of Nature truly, though
> he does not keep accurately to every feature of her.[1]

Trapp's opinion, if not his words, can be found in critic after critic
during the eighteenth century: in Leonard Welsted, Thomas
Watson, David Hume, and James Beattie, to name but a few.[2]

Dryden was fonder of Ovid and fairer to him than Trapp or
his successors. But the good qualities that Dryden saw in Ovid
were not those that the later eighteenth century could appreciate,
and the defects that he discovered were those from which it
shrank in horror. To be false to nature, luxuriant and indecorous
in thought, loose and incorrect in style—all this ensured critical
neglect and oblivion. Augustan neoclassicism was marked as
much by the eclipse of Ovid as by the recovery of Horace. In 1783
James Beattie could look back on the taste of a former age and
remark with wonder on its neglect of "Homer, Virgil, Cicero,
and all the most elegant authors," and on its preference for
"everything that was incredible and monstrous": Dares Phrygius,
Dictys Cretensis, Claudian—and Ovid.[3]

It is not surprising, then, that Ovid was infrequently trans-
lated during the eighteenth century. How infrequently may
startle some. In the case of most of Ovid's works, translations
made during the early eighteenth century became standard and
continued to be reprinted well into the nineteenth century.
Garth's edition of the *Metamorphoses*, for example, appeared for
the first time in 1717 and went through a dozen editions in the
next hundred years.[4] It was the only complete version of the
Metamorphoses published during the eighteenth century, and
just as Garth's preface repeated in a reduced and simplified form
Dryden's judgement of Ovid and threefold division of translation,[5]
so the "Garth" *Metamorphoses* was built around a core of Dryden's
translations. No other of the eighteen contributors (they included

Addison, Congreve, Gay, Pope—for the episode of Dryope in Book Nine—Nicholas Rowe, and Nahum Tate) translated as much as Dryden, who provided nearly a quarter of the whole.

Most of Ovid's other works, if they appeared in translation at all during the eighteenth century, appeared in similar collaborative editions, with Dryden the principal contributor. The version of the *Ars Amatoria* and *Remedia Amoris* by Dryden, Congreve, and Nahum Tate was reprinted ten times in the century after its first appearance in 1709. An assemblage of *Ovid's Epistles: with his Amours. Translated into English verse, by the most eminent hands*, Dryden's and Pope's chief among them, was published by Jacob Tonson in 1725. Further combined editions appeared in 1729, 1736, 1748, 1761, 1826, and 1833. The *Heroides* without the *Amores* had appeared first in 1681; the eighth edition of this translation came in 1712, and with Sir Carr Scrope's translation of "Sappho to Phaon" replaced by that of Pope, it was reprinted in 1716, 1720, 1795, and 1808.

Otherwise there is hardly anything: no translation of the *Epistulae ex Ponto* between Wye Saltonstall's in 1639 and R. Mongan's crib of 1848, no translation of the *Ibis* after John Jones in 1658. The *Fasti* did attract the attention of antiquarians: *Ovid's Fasti, or the Romans Sacred Calendar, translated in English Verse* by William Massey, "master of a boarding-school at Wandsworth," appeared in 1757.

These are not all the translations of Ovid published during the eighteenth century. Translations of separate books or episodes, translations in the *Town and Country Magazine*,[6] translations "For the Use and Entertainment of the Ladies of Great Britain,"[7] translations made by young gentlemen of the University of Cambridge, or by schoolmasters for the edification of their charges—all become blurred after a day or so in the library into one translation, and that not worth a second reading. There seems to have been a general feeling in the eighteenth century that Ovid had been done, and that all translations had to be measured not against Ovid but against the basically Drydenic versions published early in the century. Commenting on one version, the *Monthly Review* noted that "What poetry there may be in the style, is evidently taken from former poetical translations of Ovid. . . . [T]his editor acknowledges, his expressions are chiefly borrowed from Dryden, Addison, Pope, etc. etc." The *Analytical Review* found another fallen short of the inevitable standard: "We can by no means rank this poetical version with the labours of a Dryden, or a Pope."[8]

Not translation proper, but imitation, burlesque, and parody were the modes through which the century after Dryden made Ovid English. The three modes tend to merge into one another, and the difference between burlesque and parody especially is largely a matter of tone.[9] Swift's *Baucis and Philemon*, for example, combines elements of all three. Its subtitle proclaims it to be "Imitated, From the Eighth Book of OVID," and its substance is as close to *Metamorphoses* 8.611–724 as *London* or *The Vanity of Human Wishes* to their originals in Juvenal. Like Johnson's imitations, also, *Baucis and Philemon* has a moralizing purpose: to satirize materialism in the church and clergy. On the other hand, its merry iambic trimeter and its emphasis on lowlife and everyday things, beggars and piss-pots, contrast with its classic original and make Swift's poem into a burlesque on Ovid.[10]

To treat eighteenth-century burlesques, parodies, and imitations of Ovid would expand this book beyond both its chronological and its material limits. Yet some mention, at least, of these other modes has been necessary. Taken with the dearth of new translations of Ovid during the eighteenth century, they are symptomatic of the change in sensibility wrought by Dryden. His translations and criticism summed up and gave final expression to the development of style as the most important element in translation, and they changed the way people read Ovid. After Dryden, when Ovid was held up to nature, he was found wanting, and when he was judged for style the verdict was no more favorable. What remained but to acknowledge that, if translation of so elementary an author were needed, the existing versions, correct, faithful, and by the best hands, were enough, and that the only interesting way to treat this author in English was "not only to vary from the words and sense, but to forsake them both . . . and taking only some general hints from the original, to run division on the ground-work?"[11]

Whether seen, as this book has seen him, as the man who finished off the Renaissance tradition in translation, or regarded as the first modern translator, Dryden is the hinge upon which turns the history of translation in English literature. In the case of translations of Ovid, Dryden's importance is even greater. His version, or versions patterned on his, became the standard from which there was no deviation until recent times. There was not— has not yet been, some might say—a version with the idiosyncratic clarity of vision that informs the translations of Marlowe and Sandys.

Further, the reading of Ovid implicit in Dryden's translations and explicit in his criticism remained the dominant view not only through the eighteenth century but beyond. Neither the Romantic discovery of Greece nor the stern and moral Hellenism of the Victorians left much room for Ovid in the canon of first-rank authors. There are exceptions to this generalized picture—Walter Savage Landor's delight in Ovid comes to mind—but they do not affect Ovid's reputation.[12] Sometimes, indeed, they may reinforce our sense of the importance of Dryden. Keats's *Endymion* shows the influence of Ovid, but it is one particular Ovid, that of Sandys. Keats had to reach back over the authoritative mass of Dryden's translation ("Garth's" edition was still in print when Keats was writing *Endymion*) to seek a fresh *Metamorphoses* which would be at once antique and English.[13] Ezra Pound, hardly less a Romantic, did the same when he singled out Golding's Ovid as "the most beautiful book in the language."

The consequences for us, now, of Dryden's position in the history of translations of Ovid in English are clear. First, it is a mistake to suppose that we can read a translation of Ovid—and, by extension, of any other classical author—made before Dryden in the same way as we read one made after Dryden and the revolution in literary sensibility which he represents. If we read a translation from the sixteenth or earlier seventeenth century as though it was made on the same assumptions that Dryden held, we risk falsifying and undervaluing the older translation. Marlowe's *Ovid's Elegies* is an extreme case, a translation which can only be misread unless we are aware of and ready to use knowledge of the conventions of reading and numerology which Marlowe exploits. Sandys's *Ovid's Metamorphosis* is a subtler case, and perhaps more instructive on that account. Sandys's Renaissance Ovid, the preserver of ancient wisdom, was overtaken by the neoclassical emphasis on style and by the collapse of the

Hermetic and Neoplatonic world view upon which the translation depends, with the result that Sandys's translation was seen by Dryden and his successors as an incompletely formed attempt at the kind of style which they had brought as near to perfection as was appropriate to an author like Ovid.

Further, the need to recover Marlowe's principles of translation, and Sandys's, from behind the screen of Dryden's influence suggests a new and fruitful direction for translation studies. Translation theory has for the most part been directed toward consideration of the act of making translations, toward translation from the translator's point of view. (Again, the influence of Dryden's "Preface" to *Ovid's Epistles* can be seen.) The translations themselves have seldom attracted critical attention; when they have, they have been viewed as minor works, of interest only insofar as they illuminate the assumptions, techniques, and procedures underlying the original works of their author. *The Vanity of Human Wishes* is most interesting where, and because, it departs from its model; Pope's *Iliad* commands most attention for the light it sheds on Pope, his other works, and his way of writing. If Pope's Homer or Dryden's Virgil seem major works, it is because they are central to the original oeuvre of Dryden and Pope. Most translations are valued in proportion to the personal contribution of the translator or to the value of the translator's wholly original works.

But a translation is more than an original work in which the author has had the misfortune to tie himself to someone else's matter and design. Translations are fossilized readings; they preserve for us in an alien substance the skeleton from which we can reconstruct the way a work appeared to a reader in a remote time and place. As such, they are of special interest in a time when reading and the tradition of reading are in peril. I do not refer merely to the observable decline in literacy. The peril extends beyond literacy to literature. Reading, the experience of literature, is to a great extent self-referential. We do not come to a complex work free, unprepared, with our minds naked of expectation or understanding. Our experience of the text is determined by our previous reading, by what we have learned to do; more than that, the manner and quality of a text's existence, after a certain time, are enriched, perhaps even determined, by previous readings of it. For example: we know how to read Homer, who is as remote from us as any author of the West, because a tradition of reading Homer stretches from antiquity to the present day. If a third work of the richness and power of the *Iliad* and *Odyssey* were to come forth from the sands of Egypt, I doubt very much that we would be able to read it, at least not right away. It would be out of the tradition, and incomprehensible.

It is this foundation of high literacy on the tradition of reading that is at present in danger. Not fewer and fewer people, to be sure, but a smaller and smaller percentage of the reading public has the kind of familiarity with the tradition of Western literature that makes it possible to read a work like, say, *Lycidas,* and not merely to decipher it with the aid of footnotes. Worse, many people who do read such works read as though their readings were isolated from the tradition of reading. But to read a work from another time anew, to read it as though it were fresh-made, is not only impossible. It is destructive.

In this crisis of forgetfulness translations may offer, if not a remedy, at least a palliative. Traditions are usually insubstantial things, but in translations one tradition, the tradition of reading, takes on flesh. This is especially true of translations from Greek and Latin authors. Fashions change, but many ancient authors—Ovid is one—have been translated in every age. By studying these translations, by weighing them against one another, against their original as we read it, and against what we can discover of the knowledge and assumptions that went into making the transla-ion, we can reconstruct at least the outlines of the tradition of reading. Careful study of translations, where the artist's freedom of choice is more limited than in original composition, can help us to a fuller, more accurate, and more authoritative reading of original works.

Translations also, as I have tried to show in this book, deserve attention for themselves and not only as means to an improved understanding of original works or the literary tradition. Ever since Dryden readers and critics have assumed that style is the decisive—indeed, the only—criterion of a translation's worth. And in this century the assumption has held sway that a translation ought to function in complete independence of its original. These assumptions often take the form of crude dogmata: the better the poetry, the better the translation; anyone reading a translation ought not to be aware that what he is reading is not an original work. There are, of course, reasons for these assumptions. Dryden, as we have seen, shaped the assumption that style is all; Romanticism, we might add, strengthened its hold. As for the idea that a translation ought not to draw on or create any awareness of its original, how else to proceed in an age at once monoglot and multilingual? In the United States at least a translator cannot assume that his reader will know any language except English, and even among well-educated readers there is no common second language, shared as Latin used to be.

But neither assumption applies to translations made before Dryden. Thus there is a need to pay attention to the way in which translations may be read, and to realize that changing ideas on the nature and function of literature will have an effect on the way translations are made, and hence on the ways in which we may read them. This book has treated a few translations of one author, but there is room for more studies—of Virgil translations, for example, or of key figures like Philemon Holland, or of the relation between prose and verse translations. Larger questions also suggest themselves: what can careful studies of translation and original tell us about the act of reading in former ages, or about the uses and survival of Greek and Roman literature?

For that, in the end, is the place to which our study—perhaps at this point I should begin to say my study—has directed, or re-directed, me. The literature of the Romans, represented here by the works of Publius Ovidius Naso, may seem a curious object in these times for a reader's attention. Seen with innocent eyes, Roman literature seems at once ornate and jejune; it has so very little to say, and so much of it subordinates content to design, and design to the delights of rhetoric. But innocence out of season, as I have suggested, can be as destructive of literature as in life. Seen with knowledge as something that has been read and reread, continuously understood and misunderstood, Roman literature takes on a solidity and a strength that claim serious attention. Not merely the Romans' attempt to translate and transform Greek literature but also the successive translations and transformations of Roman literature in succeeding ages become, if we will take them into our reading, sources of the joy, despair, and wisdom for which we read. (The verbal jigsaw is there too, but that is another matter.) Precisely because it seems to say so little, Roman literature allows its readers to understand so much. Endurance and persistence in the midst of change count for a great deal, as Ovid knew.

Notes

Introduction: The Problem of Translation

1. The *loci classici* for almost all Western theorists from St. Jerome, *Epistulae* 57.5, onward are Horace, *Ars Poetica* 131–35, and Cicero, *De Optimo Genere Oratorum* 14. Cicero, however, was not attempting to lay down general principles for translation, and Horace was not talking about translation as the word is commonly understood; see C. O. Brink, *Horace on Poetry* (1971), 2: 210–11.

2. The most articulate and influential presentation of this extended idea of translation has been George Steiner, *After Babel* (1975). See also Walter Benjamin, "Die Aufgabe des Uebersetzers" (1923; most accessible to English readers in the translation by James Hynd and E. M. Valk, in *Delos* 2 [1968]: 76–99; and in *Illuminations*, ed. Hannah Arendt [New York: Harcourt, Brace, and World, 1968], pp. 69–82); Louis Kelly, *The True Interpreter* (1979); Georges Mounin, *Linguistique et Traduction* (1976), pp. 59–108; and Willard V. O. Quine, *Word and Object* (1960), pp. 148–72.

3. I. A. Richards, "Towards a Theory of Translating" (1953), p. 250.

4. Aeschylus, *The Oresteia* (1975).

5. Aeschylus, *Agamemnon* (1942).

6. Christopher Logue, *Pax: Book XIX of the Iliad* (1967), p. 15.

7. For a way into the abundant literature on this complex of ideas, see S. K. Heninger, Jr., *Touches of Sweet Harmony: Pythagorean Cosmology and Renaissance Poetics* (1974); Paul O. Kristeller, *The Philosophy of Marsilio Ficino* (1943); and Frances Yates, *Giordano Bruno and the Hermetic Tradition* (1964).

8. J. Wight Duff's summing up, *A Literary History of Rome* (written in 1909), is representative of the previous consensus:

Facility has been already noted as the great characteristic of this 'idle singer of an empty day.' His ready dexterity was the off-spring of genius tutored by rhetorical practice. Rhetoric is responsible for a large proportion of Ovid's weaknesses—for the tedious profusion of paraphrase and antithesis and *communes loci* with which he serves up a single thought, and for his straining after point, which fosters artificial *concetti*. His psychology presents no incisive introspection; his narrative no soaring imagination. Throughout, clever workmanship is more to him than a great subject—*materiam superabat opus*. (2: 443).

The most influential contributors to the modern revaluation of Ovid have been Hermann Fraenkel, *Ovid: A Poet Between Two Worlds* (1945; repr. 1956); L. P. Wilkinson, *Ovid Recalled* (1955); and Brooks Otis, *Ovid as an Epic Poet* (1966; significantly revised 1970).

1. Marlowe: The Well Agreeing File

1. Douglas Bush, "Notes on Hero and Leander," *PMLA* 44 (1929): 760–64; J. B. Steane, *Marlowe: A Critical Study* (1964), p. 291.

2. Douglas Bush, *Mythology and the Renaissance Tradition in English Poetry* (1932), pp. 70–73.

3. Conveniently accessible in *Elizabethan Narrative Verse*, ed. Nigel Alexander (1968), pp. 27–32.

4. C. S. Lewis, *English Literature of the Sixteenth Century* (1954), pp. 222–71; John Thompson, *The Founding of English Metre* (1961), pp. 33–36.

5. Postvocalic "-eth" is sometimes not counted as a syllable, but in this example neither "-eth" follows a vowel; Thompson, pp. 159–65.

6. Lines 77–84, translating *Met.* 3.407–412.

7. T. W. Baldwin, *William Shakspere's Small Latine and Lesse Greeke* (1944), 2: 417–54.

8. On this aspect of *Narcissus*, see Gordon Braden, *The Classics and English Renaissance Technique* (1978), pp. 48–49.

9. John Brinsley, *Ludus Literarius* (1627), quoted in Baldwin, 2: 386.

10. Ezra Pound's description of Golding's *Ovid* as "the most beautiful book in the language" ("The New Classics," *ABC of Reading*, London: 1934, p. 58) is probably responsible for its being one of the more over-rated. Even its undoubted influence on Shakespeare has been exaggerated; see Baldwin, 2: 430–52. The best and most accessible treatment of Golding, with full pointers to earlier literature, is now Braden, pp. 1–54.

11. Baldwin, 2: 448; Roma Gill, "Snakes Leape by Verse," in *Christopher Marlowe*, ed. Brian Morris (1968), pp. 135–50.

12. "To the Reader," lines 179–82; *Ovid's Metamorphoses: The Arthur*

Golding Translation (1965), pp. 427–28.

13. Steane, p. 287.

14. *Tristia* 3.3, 1–6; Churchyard is cited from the Roxburghe Club edition (1816), n.p. On "dalliance with the letter," see Baldwin, 2: 38.

15. Thompson, p. 33.

16. First published in Thomas Park's *Nugae Antiquae* (1804), 2: 372–89.

17. For a possible influence of Churchyard's dramatic writings on Marlowe's, see Alwin Thaler, "Churchyard and Marlowe," *MLN* 38 (1923), 89–92.

18. On the *Heroides* in general, see Howard Jacobson, *Ovid's Heroides* (1974).

19. Thompson, pp. 65–67.

20. P. 98v, translating *Heroides* 16.13–16.

21. P. 75r, translating *Heroides* 13.9–11.

22. See Wilkinson, *Ovid Recalled*, pp. 423–27.

23. On the date, see *The Complete Works of Christopher Marlowe*, Fredson Bowers, ed. (1973), 2: 309–14; Roma Gill and Robert Krueger, "The Early Editions of Marlowe's Elegies and Davies's Epigrams: Sequence and Authority," *The Library* 26 (1971), 242–49; and *The Poems of Christopher Marlowe*, Millar Maclure, ed. (1968), pp. xxxii–xxxiii.

24. I quote from E. J. Kenney's Oxford Classical Text. The Renaissance vulgate, and Marlowe's text, had *erat* for *erit*.

25. The *locus classicus* for the *militia amoris* theme is *Amores* 1.9.

26. G. Karl Galinsky, "The Triumph-Theme in Augustan Elegy," *Wiener Studien* 82 (1969): 91–94.

27. *Mens Bona* = "Good Intention," or, as Marlowe translates it, "Good Meaning"; cf. *Jew of Malta* 4.2, 7 (Barabas to Ithamore): "Yet, if he knew our meanings, could he 'scape?"

28. Marlowe's text had "Terror" for "Error" in line 35.

29. Douglass S. Parker, "The Ovidian Coda," *Arion* 8 (1969): 80–97.

30. Suetonius, *Augustus* caps. 13, 16.

31. R. M. Coogan, "Petrarch's *Trionfi* and the English Renaissance," *Studies in Philology* 67 (1970): 306–27.

32. On the structure of Latin elegiac verse, see Maurice Platnauer, *Latin Elegiac Verse* (1951), and L. P. Wilkinson, *Golden Latin Artistry* (1963), pp. 118–34.

33. Gill, p. 41.

34. Emphasis mine. On Marlowe's use of Dominicus Niger, see my "Marlowe, Dominicus Niger, and Ovid's *Amores*," *Notes and Queries* 225 (1980): 315–18.

2. Marlowe: Inexcusable Pythagorisme

1. See the works cited above, chapter 1, n. 23.

2. "Usually assigned to c. 1594–5," Marlowe, *Complete Works* 2: 309.

3. Steane, *Marlowe*, pp. 289–91.

4. There is no need to decide here or perhaps anywhere whether or not Corinna was a real person; see J. P. Sullivan, "Two Problems in Roman Love Elegy," *Transactions of the American Philological Society* 92 (1961): 522–28; Gordon Williams, *Tradition and Originality in Roman Poetry* (1968), pp. 538–42. Those who wish to believe in Corinna's reality may comfort themselves with E. de Saint Denis, "Le Malicieux Ovide," in *Ovidiana* (1958), pp. 185–90; Peter Green, *Essays in Antiquity* (1960), pp. 118–21, and the introduction to Professor Green's *Ovid: The Erotic Poems* (1982).

5. S. Bertman, "Duality in Ovid, *Amores* 1.5," *Liverpool Classical Monthly* 3 (1978): 227–29; W.S.M. Nicoll, "Ovid, *Amores* I.5," *Mnemosyne* 30 (1977): 40–48.

6. Steane, p. 291.

7. Alistair Fowler, *Triumphal Forms: Structural Patterns in Elizabethan Poetry* (1970), p. 23. See also Christopher Butler, *Number Symbolism* (1970), and R. G. Peterson, "Critical Calculations: Measure and Symmetry in Literature," *PMLA* 91 (1976): 367–75.

8. A. Kent Hieatt, *Short Time's Endless Monument* (1960); Alastair Fowler, *Spenser and the Numbers of Time* (1964); M. A. Wickert, "Structure and Ceremony in Spenser's *Epithalamion*," *ELH* 35 (1968): 135–57.

9. Ben Jonson, *Works*, eds. C. H. Herford, P. Simpson and E. M. Simpson, (1925–52); 8: 391; cf. Fowler, *Triumphal Forms*, p. 70.

10. Sir Thomas Browne, *The Garden of Cyrus*, chapter 5, in *Religio Medici, and Other Works*, ed. L. C. Martin (1964), p. 169.

11. Heninger, pp. 70–84.

12. Aristotle, *Metaphysics* 986a, 9–11.

13. Plotinus, *Enneads* 5.5, 6, p. 408, in the translation by Stephen MacKenna (1962); Marsilio Ficino, *Platonica Theologica de Immortalitate Animorum* IV.1 = *Theologie Platonicienne de l'Immortalite des Ames*, ed. Raymond Marcel (1964), 2: 154–55: *vult enim* [sc., Pythagoras] Ἀπολλονα *dici, quasi* ἄπλον *quod significat simplicem, et quasi* ἀπὸ πολλῶν, *quod significat semotum a multitudine.*

14. Fowler, *Triumphal Forms* p. 185 and n. 2, with authorities cited there; cf. also Joannes Martinus, *Arithmetica* (Paris: 1526), fol. 16r, reproduced in Heninger, p. 70.

15. *Odes* 3.30, 1–2; see Fowler, *Triumphal Forms* pp. 188–90, for other examples of pyramidal structure and reference in poetry.

16. Steane, p. 301.

17. It antedates also the third-century cult of Sol Invictus and the identification of that god with the Roman emperors; see, e.g., Dio of Prusa, "Third Discourse on Kingship," 73–85, and H. P. L'Orange, *Studies on the Iconography of Cosmic Kingship* (1953).

18. Ptolemy, *Tetrabiblos* 4.10; *Almagest* 9.1.

19. I have quoted the English version of Richard Linche, *The Fountaine of Ancient Fiction* (1599), E3r = Vincenzo Cartari, *Le Imagini dei Dei degli Antichi* (Venice: 1571), G2r.

3. George Sandys: A Translator between Two Worlds

1. Susan M. Kingsbury, ed. *Records of the Virginia Company of London*, quoted in Richard Beale Davis, *George Sandys: Poet Adventurer* (1955), p. 140.

2. No copy of the first edition of Books 1–5 is extant, but the translation was entered in the Stationers' Register in 1621. A second edition, the only known copy of which is in the Folger Library, appeared in the same year; Davis, pp. 201–3.

3. Davis, pp. 209–14. My own collation of Book 5 in the 1621 (represented by the third edition of 1623), 1626, and 1632 versions confirmed his conclusions.

4. Davis, p. 208.

5. Davis P. Harding, *Milton and the Renaissance Ovid* (1946), pp. 24–25.

6. *Ovid's Metamorphosis Englished, Mythologized, and Represented in Figures...by* G[eorge] S[andys] (1632), p. 20 (Galileo's glasses), and p. 194 (the rattlesnake). Hereafter, references in the form 1632, p. —, are to this edition.

7. See especially Lisa Jardine, *Francis Bacon: Discovery and the Art of Discourse* (1974); Paolo Rossi, *Francesco Bacone, dalla magia alla scienza* (1957) = *Francis Bacon: From Magic to Science*, tr. S. Rabinovitch (1968).

8. 1632, "To the most High and Mightie Prince Charles, King of Great Britaine, France, and Ireland."

9. For a more detailed discussion of Sandys's sources, see Davis, pp. 218–19.

10. Sandys, 1632, pp. 65–66. Francis Bacon, *The Works of Francis Bacon*, eds. James Spedding, Robert L. Ellis, and Douglas D. Heath (1858), 6: 634. All citations of Bacon are to this edition, hereafter *Works*.

11. Grace Eva Hunter, "The Influence of Francis Bacon on the Commentary of Ovid's *Metamorphoses* by George Sandys" (1949).

12. *Advancement of Learning* 1.2, 4 = *Works* 3: 271–72.

13. Extended discussion of myth appear in *Cogitationes de Scientia Humana* (written ca. 1605 but not published until 1857), *The Advancement of Learning* (1605), *De Sapientia Veterum* (1609), *De Augmentis Scientiarum* (finished in 1622 but not published until the following year), and *De Principiis atque Originibus secundum Fabulas Cupidinis et Coeli* (written perhaps in 1623 or 1624 and published in 1653).

14. Cervantes, *Don Quixote*, Part 2, chapter 22.

15. A certain amount of controversy attaches to the question whether Bacon's views on the purpose of myth changed considerably or hardly at all between the *Advancement of Learning* and the *De Sapientia Veterum*; see Barbara C. Garner, "Francis Bacon, Natalis Comes, and the Mythological Tradition," *Journal of the Warburg and Courtauld Institutes* 33 (1970): 264–91, esp. 268ff., for a detailed discussion with references to earlier literature.

16. *Advancement of Learning*, 2.4, 1 = *Works* 3: 345.

17. "Here therefore is the first distemper of learning, when men study words and not matter," *Advancement of Learning* 1.4, 3 = *Works* 3: 284. On Bacon's view of the history of knowledge, see Garner, pp. 277-78.

18. *Works* 3: 222.

19. Proemium to *Instauratio Magna* = *Works* 4: 7.

20. Rossi, pp. 162-74.

21. As demonstrated by Jardine (above, n. 7).

22. On Bacon's account of Cupid, see Howard B. White, *Antiquity Forgot: Essays on Shakespeare, Bacon, and Rembrandt* (1978), pp. 109-36.

23. Although Bacon attributes the myth to unspecified *poetae*, all the features of his account can be found in Hesiod's *Theogony* or the Orphic *Argonautica*, except for the suggestion that Cupid hatched from the egg of Night. This is a fancy of Aristophanes, *Birds* 695. (*A nonnullis traditur*, says Bacon.) Hesiod, "Orpheus," and Aristophanes, with Plato (*Phaedrus*), are the first four authors cited by Natalis Comes in his account of Cupid, *Mythologiae* 4.14. On Comes as Bacon's principal source, see C. W. Lemmi, *The Classical Deities in Bacon: A Study in Mythological Symbolism* (1933), pp. 55-72.

24. Jardine, pp. 63-75.

25. *Works* 3: 86.

26. Garner, p. 281; *Works* 4: 318.

27. . . . *nimirum ut in inventis novis et ab opinionibus vulgaribus et penitus abstrusis, aditus ad intellectum magis facilis et benignus per parabolas quaeratur, De Sapientia Veterum* praef. = *Works* 6: 628.

28. *De Rerum Natura* 2.600-603.

29. 1632, p. 20.

30. 1632, p. 29.

31. 1632, p. 67.

32. 1632, p. 100.

33. On Machiavellianism in Bacon's mythology, see Rossi, pp. 110-12.

34. 1632, p. 101.

35. 1632, p. 71.

36. Comes says (I quote from the edition published at Lyon in 1605, p. 138), *Sacer est illi* [sc., *Iunoni*] *pavo, quod superbum, quod ambitiosum, quod alta petens, utpote aereo temperamento animal, quod variis coloribus ornatum, quod multos habet oculos; quia superbi sunt, ambitiosi, rerum arduarum appetentes, qui divitiarum Deam habent tutelarem, quos multos homines observare necesse est ad rerum suarum custodiam.*

37. 1632, p. 263.

38. 1632, p. 26.

39. 1632, p. 217.

40. 1632, p. 359.

41. 1632, p. 19.

42. *Works* 6: 719-20, 646.

43. 1632, p. 111.

44. *Works* 6: 733, 658.

45. The usual version of the Prometheus myth makes Prometheus's gift of fire to mankind the cause of his punishment. Bacon's source for the story about Minerva, as for much of the rest of his account of Prometheus, was Natalis Comes, *Mythologiae* 4.6. Comes attributes the story to Duris the Samian (ca. 340–ca. 260 B.C.). Duris did not survive from antiquity, and Comes's ultimate source was probably the scholiast on Apollonius Rhodius 2.1249 = Felix Jacoby, *Die Fragmente der griechischen Historiker* (1923), ii.A.76, fr. 77.

46. Davis, p. 92.

47. 1632, p. 319. I have consulted Sabinus in *P. Ovidii Metamorphosis, seu fabulae poeticae: earumque interpretatio ethica, physica & historica Georgii Sabini* (1589). Sandys might, of course, have taken the story directly from Livy, but to have done so would be contrary to his usual practice.

48. 1632, p. 320; I have consulted Regius in *P. Ovidii Nasonis poete ingeniosissimi Metamorphoseos libri xv. In eosdem libros Raphaelis Regii luculentissime enarrationes* (1560). Compare Sandys's note with Regius's:

Now the strife between the Aetolians and Acarnanians (whose countryes are watered by that River) concerning their bounders (arbitrated for want of umpires by the sword, wherein the stronger prevailed) was the ground of this fiction of *Hercules* his subduing of *Achelous: Deianira* the daughter of *Oeneus* (for it should seeme the *Aetolians* had the better) the reward of his victory.	Bella inter Aetolos & Acarnanes vicinos ciebat [sc., Achelous]. Cumque arbitrii nulli essent, armis non iudicio decertabant. Victoriam vero reportabant qui plus viribus valebant. Quare cum Hercules fluvium damnose labentem aggeribus fossis intra alveum cohibuisset tanquam debellare: Acheloum victoriae praemium reportavit Oenei filiae Deianirae nuptias.

49. 1632, p. 481.

50. *A Learned Summary*, p. 3r.

51. Bush, *Mythology and the Renaissance Tradition*, p. 245.

52. See M.L.W. Laistner, *Thought and Letters in Western Europe, A.D. 500 to 900* (1957), pp. 34–53; E. K. Rand, *Founders of the Middle Ages* (1928). Sandys cites Tertullian on this topic, 1632, p. 29.

53. See Ernst Cassirer, *The Platonic Renaissance in England* (1953), pp. 42–49.

54. George Chapman, "To M. Harriots," accompanying *Achilles Shield* = *The Poems of George Chapman*, ed. Phyllis Brooks Bartlett (1941), p. 382; see also Millar Maclure, *Chapman: A Critical Study* (1966), p. 165.

55. George Chapman, "Epistle Dedicatory" to the *Iliads* = *Chapman's Homer*, ed. Allardyce Nicoll (1957) 1: 5.

56. Bush, *Mythology and the Renaissance Tradition*, p. 199.

57. On these poems see William Keach, *Elizabethan Erotic Narratives* (1977).

58. The term "metaphysical" would have to be abandoned if it weren't so useful. See, among others, Jean-Jacques Denouain, *Thèmes et Formes de la Poésie "Métaphysique"* (1956); Joseph Anthony Mazzeo, "A Critique of Some Modern Theories of Metaphysical Poetry," *Modern Philology* 50 (1952): 88–96; Rosemund Tuve, *Elizabethan and Metaphysical Imagery: Renaissance Poetic and Twentieth-Century Critics* (1947); F. R. Leavis, "English Poetry in the Seventeenth Century," *Scrutiny* 4 (1935): 236–56; and W. Bradford Smith, "What is Metaphysical Poetry," *Sewanee Review* 42 (1934): 261–72.

59. See Liselotte Dieckmann, "Renaissance Hieroglyphics," *Comparative Literature* 9 (1957): 308–21; Rosemary Freeman, *English Emblem Books* (1948); D. C. Allen, *Mysteriously Meant* (1981).

60. *Ludovico Ariosto's Orlando Furioso, translated into English heroical verse by Sir John Harington (1591)*, ed. Robert McNulty (1972), p. 17.

61. 1632, "To the Reader."

62. John Aubrey, *"Brief Lives"*, ed. Andrew Clark (1898) 1: 36, 2: 166.

63. Quoted in Michael Hunter, *John Aubrey and the Realm of Learning* (1975), p. 20.

4. Sandys's Style: The Sentence Inforceth

1. 1632, p. 189.

2. The comparison of sense contracted by meter to sound passing through a trumpet is a Renaissance commonplace used by, e.g., Montaigne at the beginning of *Essays* 1.26, "Of the Education of Children." Montaigne correctly attributes it to the Stoic Cleanthes, although his source was Seneca, *Epistulae Morales* 108, 10 = fr. 487, in J. von Arnim, *Stoicorum Veterum Fragmenta* (1905), 1: 109.

3. Bodl. Ashmole MS 47, no. 80, quoted in Davis, p. 223.

4. On Sandys's contribution, see especially Ruth C. Wallerstein, "The Development of the Rhetoric and Metre of the Heroic Couplet 1642–45," *PMLA* 50 (1935): 166–209; Mario Praz, *La Poesia di Pope e le sue Origini* (1948), pp. 67–69; Geoffrey Tillotson, *On the Poetry of Pope* (1950), pp. 63–78.

5. On the fate of this image in the later seventeenth century, see John Hollander, *The Untuning of the Sky* (1961).

6. 1632, p. 70.

7. 1632, p. 446.

8. See n. 4, above.

9. 1632, pp. 201, 271.

10. *Metamorphoses* 2.626–7.

11. Davis, p. 212.

12. 1621 edition (in the printing of 1623), p. 134; 1626 edition, p. 101;

1632, p. 182.

13. 1632, p. 179.

14. H. Wood, "Beginnings of the 'Classical' Heroic Couplet in England," *American Journal of Philology* 11 (1890): 74–75.

15. 1632, p. 203.

16. 1632, p. 371.

17. Davis, p. 212.

18. "The Arte of English Poesie," in *Elizabethan Critical Essays*, ed. G. Gregory Smith (1904), 2: 8.

19. *Metamorphoses* 2.700–707. Modern editions read *erunt* for the first *erant* in 703, but I have quoted the Renaissance vulgate.

20. 1632, p. 60.

21. Anthony Blackwall, *An Introduction to the Classics* (1718), p. 202.

22. John Dryden, "A Discourse Concerning the Original and Progress of Satire," in *Of Dramatic Poesy and Other Critical Essays*, ed. George Watson (1962), 2: 151.

23. John Dryden, "Dedication to the *Aeneis*," *Of Dramatic Poesy* 2: 238.

24. See Seneca Rhetor, *Controversiae* 2.2.

25. 1632, p. 204, translating *Metamorphoses* 6.118–20.

26. On the episode in general, see J. M. Frecaut, "La métamorphose de Niobé chez Ovide (*Met.* VI, 301–312)," *Latomus* 39 (1980): 129–43.

27. *Metamorphoses* 6.280–86.

28. 1632, p. 207.

29. Dryden, "Dedication to the *Aeneis*," *Of Dramatic Poesy* 2: 245.

30. See my "Marlowe, Dominicus Niger, and Ovid's *Amores*," pp. 315–18.

31. Wallerstein, p. 187.

32. 1632, p. 249.

33. 1632, p. 243.

34. George Sandys, *Christ's Passion, A Tragedy; with Annotations* (1687), fol. A4r.

35. 1632, p. 188.

36. 1632, p. 37.

37. 1632, p. 85.

38. 1632, p. 89.

39. John Barsby, *Ovid, Greece & Rome*, New Surveys in the Classics, 12 (1978): 36–37.

40. From the long prologue spoken by Christ, 1687 edition, fol. B3v, translating Grotius's

Quid illa sanctis semper adversa & Deo
Hostilis Erebi dira pallentis lues
Non pulsa nostris legibus mortalium
Habitata linquit pectora & vocem tremuit?
Post opera tanta non satis Christo fuit
Prodesse viris. victor ingenti manu

Fregi silentum regna, & inferum chaos.

41. See especially Tillotson, pp. 66–73.

42. 1632, pp. 82–83; emphasis on epithets, except for "Stygian," mine.

43. Douglas Bush, *English Literature in the Earlier Seventeenth Century* (1945), p. 75.

44. From the preface to the Authorized Version.

5. Dryden: Translation as Style

1. William Frost, *Dryden and the Art of Translation* (1955), p. 1. Unless otherwise indicated, citations of Dryden's poetry are to the California edition, *The Works of John Dryden*, eds. Edward Niles Hooker, H. T. Swedenberg, Jr., Vinton A. Dearing, et al. (1956–), hereafter *Works. Fables Ancient and Modern* is cited from vol. 4 of James Kinsley's edition (1958). Dryden's prose and verse criticism is cited from the Everyman edition, *Of Dramatic Poesy and Other Critical Essays*, ed. George Watson (1962).

2. Dryden on Ovid: *Of Dramatic Poesy* 2: 163. The eighteenth-century critic is Oldmixon, in *The Arts of Logic and Rhetorick* (1728), p. 291, quoted at *Works* 1: 324: "Dryden seems to have enter'd as far into the Genius of Ovid as any of his Translators. That Genius has more of Equality with his own than Virgil's; and, consequently, his versions of Ovid are more perfect than those of Virgil."

3. See, for example, L. Proudfoot, *Dryden's Aeneid and its Seventeenth Century Predecessors* (1960); Robert M. Adams, *Proteus, His Lies, His Truth: Discussions of Literary Translation* (1973); Norman Austin, "Translation as Baptism: A Study of Dryden's Lucretius," *Arion* 7 (1968): 576–602. Most studies of Dryden's Ovid translations have been concerned with their sources and borrowings from previous translators or with their influence on later works. Much of this material is collected in the notes to the translations in *Works*.

4. The similarities and differences between Pope's classicism and that of the Renaissance have yet to be fully explored; see R. G. Peterson, "Renaissance Classicism in Pope's *Dunciad*," *Studies in English Literature* 15 (1975): 431–45.

5. Dryden, *Of Dramatic Poesy* 2: 270.

6. Dryden, *Of Dramatic Poesy* 2:164.

7. Dryden, *Of Dramatic Poesy* 2: 270.

8. It was first published in the folio edition of the *Works* of Drummond of Hawthornden, Edinburgh, 1711; see *Critical Essays of the Seventeenth Century*, ed. J. E. Spingarn (1908), 1: 182.

9. Spingarn, 1: xxi.

10. Spinarn, 1: 142.

11. "Apologie for Poetry" in *The Prose Works of Sir Philip Sidney*, ed. Albert Feuillerat (1962), 3: 10.

12. *Poetics* 1447b.

13. *Poetics* 1460b.

14. *Poetics* 1451b.

15. Pope, *Essay on Criticism* 68–73.

16. Sidney "Apologie for Poetry", p. 8.

17. *Essay on Criticism* 315–19.

18. Bacon, *Advancement of Learning*, Book 1 = *Works* 3: 283.

19. Bacon, *Advancement of Learning* Book 2 = *Works* 3: 343.

20. For Dryden's borrowings from all these, see the notes to the California edition. I am not convinced that he made much use of Marlowe's version of the *Amores*. The evidence cited in the California edition (*Works* 4: 757–59) for his use of Marlowe in *Amores* 1.1 includes nothing that cannot reasonably be assigned to coincidence. The traces of Marlowe in Dryden's version of *Amores* 1.4 are stronger, but still not as conclusive as the indubitable signs of the anonymous version of 1683 in 1.1. There seem to be no reminiscences of Marlowe at all in Dryden's version of 2.19.

21. On French neoclassicism, see René Bray, *La Formation de la Doctrine Classique en France* (1931). Useful remarks on English neoclassicism can be found in Walter Jackson Bate, *The Burden of the Past and the English Poet* (1970), and Reuben Brower, *Alexander Pope* (1959). For an account of non-French sources of English neoclassicism, see James William Johnson, *The Formation of English Neo-Classical Thought* (1967). The question of French critics' influence on Dryden, and its overestimation, is treated in the important work of John Aden, "Dryden and Boileau: The Question of Critical Influence," *Studies in Philology* 50 (1953): 491–509; "Dryden and Saint Evremond," *Comparative Literature* 6 (1954): 232–39; "Dryden, Corneille, and the *Essay of Dramatic Poesy*," *Review of English Studies* 6 (1955): 147–56.

22. Johnson, pp. 138–41; Butler, pp. 50–51.

23. Dryden, *Of Dramatic Poesy* 2: 219, 1: 265.

24. Swift, "To Stella, Visiting me in my Sickness (1720)," 37–42.

25. But not entirely there; for the Renaissance use of visual material, see Charles Mitchell, "Archaeology and Romance in Renaissance Italy," in *Italian Renaissance Studies*, ed. E. F. Jacob (1960), pp. 455–83; Erna Mandowsky and Charles Mitchell, "Introduction" to *Pirro Ligorio's Roman Antiquities* (1963); Roberto Weiss, *The Renaissance Discovery of Classical Antiquity* (1969); Peterson, "Renaissance Classicism," pp. 436–38.

26. "Preface" to *Ovid's Epistles*, Dryden, *Of Dramatic Poesy* 1: 270.

27. Roscommon, *Essay on Translated Verse* 14–15.

28. Spingarn 1: 51.

29. Spingarn 1: 50.

30. Dryden, *Of Dramatic Poesy* 2: 14–17; for an account of the poem's background and an explanation of its allusions, see *Works* 2: 379–83. It will be evident from what follows that I do not agree with the California editors' statement (p. 381) that Denham, in *Progress of Learning* (1668), was the first to treat of the origins of poetry, and that I find in lines 14–15 of Roscommon's *Essay* an additional and more direct source

for Dryden's garden imagery. Earl Miner, "Dryden and the Issue of Human Progress," *Philological Quarterly* 40 (1961): 120–29, relates Dryden's poem to seventeenth-century controversies over progress.

31. Roscommon, *Essay* 14–15: "The noblest Fruits, Transplanted, in our Isle / With early Hope and fragrant Blossoms smile." The image may also owe something to Denham's lines in "To Sir Richard Fanshaw upon his Translation of Pastor Fido" (1648): "Nor ought a Genius less than his that writ, / Attempt Translation; for transplanted wit, / All the defects of air and soil doth share."

32. See n. 18., above.

33. Virgil, *Eclogue* 3.84–87; *Works* 2: 382.

34. Dryden, *Of Dramatic Poesy* 1: 190–91.

35. Dedication to *Examen Poeticum*, Dryden, *Of Dramatic Poesy* 2: 164.

6. Dryden: Style in Translation

1. "Preface" to *Ovid's Epistles*, in Dryden, *Of Dramatic Poesy* 1: 270.

2. Dryden, *Of Dramatic Poesy* 1: 201.

3. Dryden, *Of Dramatic Poesy*: smoothly and easily, 1: 22; turns, 2: 151, 279; the bounds of good taste, 1: 272; failure to observe decorum, 2: 263; inferior to Chaucer, 2: 277; to Virgil, 2: 238.

4. "Dedication" to *Examen Poeticum*, Dryden, *Of Dramatic Poesy* 2: 163.

5. See the comments on this passage by F. Bömer, ed., *Ovid: Die Metamorphosen*, vol. 1 (1969); and A. G. Lee, ed., *Ovid: Metamorphoses I* (1953).

6. Mark Van Doren, *John Dryden: A Study of His Poetry* (1960), pp. 94–114, 208–40.

7. *Works* 2: 374.

8. Miltonic echoes: 1.114, 132, 212, 226, 997; Christian coloring: 1.155 (God's mercy), 241 (original sin), 506–7 (altars and saints), 510–11 (forgiveness), 512 (rebirth), 521 (relics), 536–37 (miracles). See *Works* ad loc.

9. *Works*, vol. 1, p. 328.

10. Dryden, *Of Dramatic Poesy* 1: 99.

11. Parker, pp. 80–97.

12. I think that the double letters are genuine; that the ninth, which is not so bad that Ovid couldn't have written it, is probably genuine; and that the fifteenth is suspect. The most recent arguments against Ovid's authorship are E. Courtney, "Ovidian and Non-Ovidian *Heroides*," *Bulletin of the Institute of Classical Studies* 12 (1965): 63–66; and D.W.T.C. Vessey, "Notes on Ovid, *Heroides* 9," *Classical Quarterly* 19 (1969): 348–61. On the other side, see Valerie A. Tracy, "The Authenticity of *Heroides* 16–21," *Classical Journal* 66 (1971): 328–30; and the still persuasive statistics in Sereno Burton Clark, "The Authorship and the Date of the

Double Letters in Ovid's *Heroides*," *Harvard Studies in Classical Philology* 19 (1908): 121–55.

13. Dryden, *Of Dramatic Poesy* 2: 164.

14. Dryden, *Of Dramatic Poesy* 2: 163.

Epilogue: Sweet Ovid's Ghost

1. Joseph Trapp, "Beauty of Thought in Poetry," in *Eighteenth-Century Critical Essays*, ed. Scott Elledge (1961), p. 243.

2. Elledge: Welsted, p. 347; Watson, p. 795; Hume, p. 810; Beattie, p. 921. See also Samuel Garth's "Preface" to his edition of *Ovid's Metamorphoses Translated by the Most Eminent Hands* (1717), p. i.

3. Elledge, p. 921.

4. The *British Museum Catalogue* shows editions in 1717, 1724, 1727, 1751 (the fifth edition), 1794, 1807, 1810, 1812, 1813, 1815, and 1826.

5. 1717 ed., pp. i, xix.

6. E.g., 1769, pp. 159–60; 1760, pp. 50, 553; 1792, pp. 90–91.

7. *Ovids Metamorphosis epitomized in an English poetical Style, For the Use and Entertainment of the Ladies of Great Britain*, London, 1761.

8. *Monthly Review*, February 1761, 154–55; *Analytical Review*, October 1791, 208.

9. If, indeed, any useful distinction can be drawn at all; see George Kitchin, *A Survey of Burlesque and Parody in English* (1931), pp. xx–xxii.

10. On satire in *Baucis and Philemon*, see Eric Rothstein, "Jonathan Swift as Jupiter: 'Baucis and Philemon,'" in *The Augustan Milieu: Essays presented to Louis A. Landa* (1970), pp. 205–24.

11. Dryden, "Preface" to *Ovid's Epistles*, in *Of Dramatic Poesy* 1: 268.

12. Landor's opinion of Ovid: *The Complete Works of Walter Savage Landor*, eds. T. E. Welby and S. Wheeley (1927–36), 7: 240; 9: 171, 200.

13. See the notes to *Endymion* in E. de Selincourt's edition of *The Poems* (1961), pp. 410–53; and J. Grundy, "Keats and Sandys," *Notes and Queries* 200 (1955), 82–83.

Bibliography

Adams, Robert M. *Proteus, His Lies, His Truth: Discussions of Literary Translation.* New York: W. W. Norton, 1973.

Aden, John. "Dryden and Boileau: The Question of Critical Influence." *Studies in Philology* 50 (1953): 491–509.

_____. "Dryden and Saint Evremond." *Comparative Literature* 6 (1954): 232–39.

_____. "Dryden, Corneille, and the *Essay of Dramatic Poesy.*" *Review of English Studies* 6 (1955): 147–56.

Aeschylus. *Agamemnon.* Translated by Richmond Lattimore. In *The Complete Greek Tragedies.* Chicago: University of Chicago Press, 1942.

_____. *The Oresteia.* Translated by Robert Fagles. New York: Viking, 1975.

Alexander, Nigel, ed. *Elizabethan Narrative Verse.* Cambridge, Mass.: Harvard University Press, 1968.

Allen, D. C. *Mysteriously Meant.* Baltimore: Johns Hopkins University Press, 1981.

Aubrey, John. *"Brief Lives," chiefly of Contemporaries, set down by John Aubrey, between the Years 1669 & 1696.* Edited by Andrew Clark. 2 vols. Oxford: Clarendon Press, 1898.

Austin, Norman. "Translation as Baptism: A Study of Dryden's Lucretius." *Arion* 7 (1968): 576–602.

Bacon, Francis. *The Works of Francis Bacon.* Edited by James Spedding, Robert L. Ellis, and Douglas D. Heath. 14 vols. London: Longman & Co., 1858.

Baldwin, T. W. *William Shakspere's Small Latine and Lesse Greeke.* 2 vols. Urbana: University of Illinois Press, 1944.

163

Barsby, John. *Ovid. Greece & Rome*, New Surveys in the Classics, 12. Oxford: Clarendon Press, 1978.

Bate, Walter Jackson. *The Burden of the Past and the English Poet.* Cambridge, Mass.: Harvard University Press, 1970.

Benjamin, Walter. "Die Aufgabe des Uebersetzers." Introduction to *Tableaux Parisiens*, Heidelberg, 1923. Translated by James Hynd and E. M. Valk. *Delos* 2 (1968): 76–99.

Bertman, S. "Duality in Ovid, *Amores* 1.5." *Liverpool Classical Monthly* 3 (1978): 227–29.

Betti, Emilio. "Probleme der Übersetzung und der nachbildenden Auslegung." *Deutsche Vierteljahrsschrift fur Literaturwissenschaft* 27 (1955): 489–509.

_____. *Teoria generale della interpretazione.* 2 vols. Milan: Istituto di Teoria della Interpretazione, 1955.

Blackwall, Anthony. *An Introduction to the Classics.* London, 1718.

Bömer, F., ed. *Ovid: Die Metamorphosen.* Heidelberg: Carl Winter, 1969.

Bovie, S. Palmer. "Complete Translations." *MLN* 90 (1975): 800–808.

Braden, Gordon. *The Classics and English Renaissance Technique.* New Haven: Yale University Press, 1978.

Bray, René. *La Formation de la Doctrine Classique en France.* Paris: Hachette, 1927.

Brink, C. O. *Horace on Poetry.* 2 vols. Cambridge: Cambridge University Press, 1971.

Brooks, Harold F. "The 'Imitation' in English Poetry, Especially in Formal Satire, Before the Age of Pope." *Review of English Studies* 25 (1949): 124–40.

Brower, Reuben. *Alexander Pope.* Oxford: Oxford University Press, 1959.

_____. *On Translation.* Harvard Studies in Comparative Literature, 23. Cambridge, Mass.: Harvard University Press, 1959.

Browne, Sir Thomas. *Religio Medici, and Other Works.* Edited by L. C. Martin. Oxford: Clarendon Press, 1962.

Brüggemann, Lewis W. *A View of the English Editions, Translations, and Illustrations of the Ancient Greek and Latin Authors.* 2 vols. London, 1797. Reprint. Burt Franklin Bibliography and Reference Series, 84. New York: Burt Franklin, 1975.

Bush, Douglas. *English Literature in the Earlier Seventeenth*

Century. Oxford History of English Literature, vol. 5. Oxford: Clarendon Press, 1962.

_____. *Mythology and the Renaissance Tradition in English Poetry*. Minneapolis: University of Minnesota Press, 1932.

_____. *Mythology and the Romantic Tradition in English Poetry*. Cambridge, Mass.: Harvard University Press, 1937.

_____. "Notes on *Hero and Leander*." *PMLA* 44 (1929): 760–64.

Butler, Christopher. *Number Symbolism*. London: Routledge & Kegan Paul, 1970.

Cartari, Vincenzo. *Le Imagini dei Dei degli Antichi*. Venice, 1571.

Cassirer, Ernst. *The Platonic Renaissance in England*. Austin: University of Texas Press, 1953.

Chapman, George. *Chapman's Homer*. Edited by Allardyce Nicoll. 2 vols. London: Routledge & Kegan Paul, 1957.

_____. *The Poems of George Chapman*. Edited by Phyllis Brooks Bartlett. Modern Language Association of America, General Series 12. New York: Modern Language Association, 1941.

Churchyard, Thomas. *Ovid's Tristia*. London: The Roxburghe Club, 1816.

Clark, Sereno Burton. "The Authorship and the Date of the Double Letters in Ovid's Heroides." *Harvard Studies in Classical Philology* 19 (1908): 121–55.

Coogan, R. M. "Petrarch's *Trionfi* and the English Renaissance." *Studies in Philology* 67 (1970): 306–27.

Courtney, E. "Ovidian and Non-Ovidian *Heroides*." *Bulletin of the Institute of Classical Studies* 12 (1965): 63–66.

Davis, Richard Beale. *George Sandys: Poet-Adventurer*. New York: Columbia University Press, 1955.

Denonain, Jean-Jacques. *Thèmes et Formes de la Poésie "Metaphysique."* Publications de la Faculté des Lettres d'Alger, 28. Paris: Presses Universitaires de France, 1956.

Dieckmann, Liselotte. "Renaissance Hieroglyphics." *Comparative Literature* 9 (1957): 308–21.

Dio of Prusa. *Works*. Translated by J. W. Goheen & H. L. Crosby. Loeb Classical Library. 5 vols. London: Heinemann, 1932–51.

Dryden, John. *The Works of John Dryden*. Edited by Edward Niles Hooker, H. T. Swedenberg, Jr., Vinton A. Dearing, et al. Berkeley and Los Angeles: University of California Press, 1956–.

_____. *Fables Ancient and Modern*. Edited by James Kinsley. *The Poetical Works of Dryden*, vol. 4. Oxford: Clarendon Press, 1958.

_____. *Of Dramatic Poesy and Other Critical Essays*. Edited by George Watson. Everyman's Library. 2 vols. London: J. M. Dent & Sons, 1962.

Duff, J. Wight. *A Literary History of Rome*. 3d ed. 2 vols. New York: Barnes & Noble, 1953.

Elledge, Scott, ed. *Eighteenth-Century Critical Essays*. Ithaca: Cornell University Press, 1961.

Ficino, Marsilio. *Platonica Theologica de Immortalitate Animorum IV.1 = Théologie Platonicienne de l'Immortalité des Ames*. Edited by Raymond Marcel. Paris: Les Belles Lettres, 1964.

Fowler, Alastair. *Spenser and the Numbers of Time*. London: Routledge & Kegan Paul, 1964.

_____. *Triumphal Forms: Structural Patterns in Elizabethan Poetry*. Cambridge: Cambridge University Press, 1970.

Fraenkel, Hermann. *Ovid: A Poet Between Two Worlds*. Berkeley: University of California Press, 1945. Reprinted 1956.

Frecaut, J. M. "La métamorphose de Niobé chez Ovide (*Met*, VI, 301–312)." *Latomus* 39 (1980): 129–43.

Freeman, Rosemary. *English Emblem Books*. London: Chatto & Windus, 1948.

Frost, William. *Dryden and the Art of Translation*. New Haven and London, 1955. Reprint. Hamden, Connecticut: Archon Books, 1969.

Galinsky, G. Karl. "The Triumph-Theme in Augustan Elegy." *Wiener Studien* 82 (1969): 75–107.

Garner, Barbara C. "Francis Bacon, Natalis Comes, and the Mythological Tradition." *Journal of the Warburg and Courtauld Institutes* 33 (1970): 264–91.

Garth, Samuel, ed. *Ovid's Metamorphoses Translated by the Most Eminent Hands*. London, 1717.

Gill, Roma. "Snakes Leape by Verse." In *Christopher Marlowe*, edited by Brian Morris. New York: Hill and Wang, 1968.

Gill, Roma, and Robert Krueger. "The Early Editions of Marlowe's Elegies and Davies's Epigrams: Sequence and Authority." *The Library* 26 (1971): 242–49.

Golding, Arthur. *Ovid's Metamorphoses: The Arthur Golding*

Translation. Edited by J. F. Nims. New York: Macmillan, 1965.

Green, Peter. *Essays in Antiquity*. Cleveland and New York: World Publishing Co., 1960.

————. *Ovid: The Erotic Poems*. Penguin Classics. Harmondsworth: Penguin Books, 1982.

Grundy, J. "Keats and Sandys." *Notes and Queries* 200 (1955): 82–83.

Harding, Davis P. *Milton and the Renaissance Ovid*. Illinois Studies in Language and Literature 30, no. 4. Urbana: University of Illinois Press, 1946.

Harington, John. *Ludovico Ariosto's Orlando Furioso, translated into English heroical verse by Sir John Harington (1591)*. Edited by Robert McNulty. Oxford: Clarendon Press, 1972.

Havens, Raymond D. "Changing Taste in the Eighteenth Century: A Study of Dryden's and Dodsley's Miscellanies." *PMLA* 44 (1929): 504–32.

Heninger, S. K. *Touches of Sweet Harmony: Pythagorean Cosmology and Renaissance Poetics*. San Marino, Cal.: The Huntington Library, 1974.

Hieatt, A. Kent. *Short Time's Endless Monument*. New York: Columbia University Press, 1960.

Highet, Gilbert. *The Classical Tradition*. Oxford: Clarendon Press, 1949.

Hollander, John. *The Untuning of the Sky*. Princeton: Princeton University Press, 1961.

Hunter, Grace Eva. "The Influence of Francis Bacon on the Commentary of Ovid's 'Metamorphoses' by George Sandys." Ph.D. dissertation, State University of Iowa, 1949.

Hunter, Michael. *John Aubrey and the Realm of Learning*. London: Duckworth, 1975.

Jacobson, Howard. *Ovid's Heroides*. Princeton: Princeton University Press, 1974.

Jacoby, Felix. *Die Fragmente der griechischen Historiker*. Berlin and Leiden, 1923–. Reprint and further volumes. Leiden: E. J. Brill, 1954–.

Jardine, Lisa. *Francis Bacon: Discovery and the Art of Discourse*. Cambridge: Cambridge University Press, 1974.

Johnson, James William. *The Formation of English Neo-Classical Thought*. Princeton: Princeton University Press, 1967.

Jonson, Ben. *Works*. Edited by C. H. Herford, P. Simpson, and E. M. Simpson. Oxford: Clarendon Press, 1925–52.

Keach, William. *Elizabethan Erotic Narratives: Irony and Pathos in the Ovidian Poetry of Shakespeare, Marlowe, and their Contemporaries*. Rutgers: Rutgers University Press, 1977.

Keats, John. *The Poems*. Edited by E. de Selincourt. London, 1905. Reprint. London: Methuen, 1961.

Kelly, Louis. *The True Interpreter*. Oxford: Blackwell, 1979.

Kitchin, George. *A Survey of Burlesque and Parody in English*. Edinburgh and London: Oliver & Boyd, 1931.

Kristeller, Paul O. *The Philosophy of Marsilio Ficino*. Translated by Virginia Conant. New York: Columbia University Press, 1943.

Laistner, M.L.W. *Thought and Letters in Western Europe, A.D. 500 to 900*. 2d ed. Ithaca: Cornell University Press, 1957.

Landor, Walter Savage. *The Complete Works of Walter Savage Landor*. Edited by T. E. Welby and S. Wheeler. London: Chapman and Hall, 1927–36.

Lathrop, Henry Burrowes. *Translations from the Classics into English from Caxton to Chapman 1477–1620*. Madison, 1933. Reprint. New York: Octagon Books, 1967.

Leavis, F. R. "English Poetry in the Seventeenth Century." *Scrutiny* 4 (1935): 236–56.

Lee, A. G., ed. *Ovid: Metamorphoses I*. Cambridge: Cambridge University Press, 1953.

Lemmi, C. W. *The Classical Deities in Bacon: A Study in Mythological Symbolism*. Baltimore: Johns Hopkins University Press, 1933.

Lewis, C. S. *English Literature of the Sixteenth Century, Excluding Drama*. Oxford History of English Literature, vol. 3. Oxford: Clarendon Press, 1954.

Linche, Richard. *The Fountaine of Ancient Fiction*. London, 1599.

Logue, Christopher. *Pax: Book XIX of the Iliad*. London: Rapp and Carroll, 1969. Reprinted as *War Music: An Account of Books XVI–XIX of Homer's Iliad*. London: Jonathan Cape Ltd. and Penguin Books, 1984.

L'Orange, H. P. *Studies in the Iconography of Cosmic Kingship*. Cambridge, Mass.: Harvard University Press, 1953.

Maclure, Millar. *Chapman: A Critical Study*. Toronto: University of Toronto Press, 1966.

Mandowsky, Erna, and Charles Mitchell. Introduction to *Pirro Ligorio's Roman Antiquities: The Drawings in MS XIII.B7 in the National Library in Naples*. London: Warburg Institute, 1963.

Marlowe, Christopher. *The Poems of Christopher Marlowe*. Edited by Millar Maclure. Manchester: Manchester University Press, 1968.

_____. *The Complete Works of Christopher Marlowe*. Edited by Fredson Bowers. 2 vols. Cambridge: Cambridge University Press, 1973.

Mazzeo, Joseph Anthony. "A Critique of Some Modern Theories of Metaphysical Poetry." *Modern Philology* 50 (1952): 88–96.

Miner, Earl. "Dryden and the Issue of Human Progress." *Philological Quarterly* 40 (1961): 120–29.

Mitchell, Charles. "Archaeology and Romance in Renaissance Italy." In *Italian Renaissance Studies*, edited by E. F. Jacob. London: Faber & Faber, 1960.

Moog-Grünewald, Maria. *Metamorphosen der Metamorphosen: Rezeptionsarten der ovidischen Verwandlungsgeschichten in Italien und Frankreich im XVI. und XVII. Jahrhundert*. Studien zum Fortwirken der Antike, 10. Heidelberg: Carl Winter, 1979.

Mounin, Georges. *Linguistique et Traduction*. Brussels: Dessart et Mardaga, 1976.

Nicoll, W.S.M. "Ovid, *Amores* I.5." *Mnemosyne* 30 (1977): 40–48.

Otis, Brooks. *Ovid as an Epic Poet*. Cambridge: Cambridge University Press, 1966. Rev. ed. 1970.

Ovid. *P. Ovidii Nasonis poete ingeniosissimi Metamorphoseos libri XV. In eosdem Libros Raphaelis Regii luculentissime enarrationes.* . . . Venice, 1560.

_____. *P. Ovidii Metamorphosis, seu fabulae poeticae: earumque interpretatio ethica, physica & historica Georgii Sabini*. Frankfurt, 1589.

_____. *P. Ovidii Nasonis Amores, Medicamina Faciei Femineae, Ars Amatoria, Remedia Amoris*. Edited by E. J. Kenney. Oxford Classical Texts. Oxford: Clarendon Press, 1961.

Palmer, Henrietta R. *List of English Editions and Translations of Greek and Latin Classics Printed Before 1641*. London: The

Bibliographical Society, 1911.

Park, Thomas. *Nugae Antiquae. . .by Sir John Harington, Knt.* London: Vernor & Hood, 1804.

Parker, Douglass S. "The Ovidian Coda." *Arion* 8 (1969): 80–97.

Pearcy, Lee T. "Marlowe, Dominicus Niger, and Ovid's *Amores.*" *Notes and Queries* no. 225 (1980): 315–18.

Peterson, R. G. "Critical Calculations: Measure and Symmetry in Literature." *PMLA* 91 (1976): 367–75.

————. "Renaissance Classicism in Pope's *Dunciad.*" *Studies in English Literature* 15 (1975): 431–45.

Platnauer, Maurice. *Latin Elegiac Verse.* Cambridge: Cambridge University Press, 1951.

Plotinus. *Enneads.* Translated by Stephen MacKenna. London: Faber and Faber, 1962.

Pope, Alexander. *Poetical Works.* Edited by Herbert Davis. Oxford Standard Authors. Oxford: Oxford University Press, 1966.

Pound, Ezra. *ABC of Reading.* London: G. Routledge & Sons, 1934.

Praz, Mario. *La Poesia di Pope e le sue Origini.* Rome: Edizioni dell' Ateneo, 1948.

Proudfoot, L. *Dryden's Aeneid and its Seventeenth Century Predecessors.* Manchester: Manchester University Press, 1960.

Quine, Willard V. O. *Word and Object.* Cambridge, Mass.: MIT Press, 1960.

Rand, E. K. *Founders of the Middle Ages.* Cambridge, Mass.: Harvard University Press, 1928.

Richards, I. A. "Towards a Theory of Translating." In *Studies in Chinese Thought,* ed. Arthur F. Wright. Chicago: Chicago University Press, 1953.

Roscommon, Wentworth Dillon, 4th earl of. "An Essay on Translated Verse." In *Minor English Poets 1660–1780: A Selection from Alexander Chalmers' "The English Poets,"* edited by David P. French. New York: Benjamin Blom, 1967.

Rossi, Paolo. *Francesco Bacone, dalla magia alla scienza.* Bari: Editori Laterza, 1957.

Rothstein, Eric. "Jonathan Swift as Jupiter: 'Baucis and Philemon.'" In *The Augustan Milieu: Essays Presented to Louis A. Landa,* edited by H. K. Miller, E. Robinson, and G. S. Rousseau. Oxford: Clarendon Press, 1970.

Saint Denis, E. de. "Le Malicieux Ovide." In *Ovidiana,* edited by

N. J. Herescu. Paris: Les Belles Lettres, 1958.

Sandys, George. *Christ's Passion, A Tragedy; with Annotations.* London, 1687.

_____. *Ovid's Metamorphosis Englished, Mythologized, and Represented in Figures.* Oxford: 1632.

Sidney, Sir Philip. *The Prose Works of Sir Philip Sidney,* edited by Albert Feuillarat. 2d ed. Cambridge: Cambridge University Press, 1962.

Smith, G. Gregory, ed. *Elizabethan Critical Essays.* Oxford: Clarendon Press, 1904.

Smith, W. Bradford. "What is Metaphysical Poetry?" *Sewanee Review* 42 (1934): 261–72.

Spingarn, J. E., ed. *Critical Essays of the Seventeenth Century.* 3 vols. Oxford: Clarendon Press, 1908.

Steane, J. B. *Marlowe: A Critical Study.* 2d ed. Cambridge: Cambridge University Press, 1974.

Steiner, George. *After Babel.* Oxford: Oxford University Press, 1975.

Sullivan, J. P. "Two Problems in Roman Love Elegy." *Transactions of the American Philological Society* 92 (1961): 522–28.

Swift, Jonathan. *The Writings of Jonathan Swift,* edited by Robert A. Greenberg and William Bowman Piper. Norton Critical Editions. New York: Norton, 1973.

Thaler, Alwin. "Churchyard and Marlowe." *MLN* 38 (1923): 89–92.

Thompson, John. *The Founding of English Metre.* London: Routledge & Kegan Paul, 1961.

Tillotson, Geoffrey. *On the Poetry of Pope.* 2d ed. Oxford: Clarendon Press, 1950.

Tracy, Valerie A. "The Authenticity of *Heroides* 16–21." *Classical Journal* 66 (1971): 328–30.

Tuve, Rosemund. *Elizabethan and Metaphysical Imagery: Renaissance Poetic and Twentieth-Century Critics.* Chicago: University of Chicago Press, 1947.

Van Doren, Mark. *John Dryden: A Study of his Poetry.* New York, 1920. Reprint. Bloomington and London: Indiana University Press, 1960.

Vessey, D.W.T.C. "Notes on Ovid, *Heroides* 9." *Classical Quarterly* 19 (1969): 348–61.

von Arnim, J. *Stoicorum Veterum Fragmenta*. 3 vols. Leipzig: B. J. Teubner, 1905.

Wallerstein, Ruth C. "The Development of the Rhetoric and Metre of the Heroic Couplet 1642–45." *PMLA* 50 (1935): 166–209.

Weiss, Roberto. *The Renaissance Discovery of Classical Antiquity*. New York: Humanities Press, 1969.

White, Howard B. *Antiquity Forgot: Essays on Shakespeare, Bacon, and Rembrandt*. The Hague and Boston: Martinus Nijhoff, 1978.

Wickert, M. A. "Structure and Ceremony in Spenser's *Epithalamion*." *ELH* 35 (1968): 135–57.

Wilkinson, L. P. *Golden Latin Artistry*. Cambridge: Cambridge University Press, 1963.

———. *Ovid Recalled*. Cambridge: Cambridge University Press, 1955.

Williams, Gordon. *Tradition and Originality in Roman Poetry*. Oxford: Clarendon Press, 1968.

Wood, H. "Beginnings of the 'Classical' Heroic Couplet in England." *American Journal of Philology* 11 (1890): 74–75.

Yates, Frances. *Giordano Bruno and the Hermetic Tradition*. Chicago: University of Chicago Press, 1964.

Index